Politically Exposed Persons

Stolen Asset Recovery (StAR) Initiative

Politically Exposed Persons

Preventive Measures
for the Banking Sector

Theodore S. Greenberg
Larissa Gray

Delphine Schantz
Carolin Gardner
Michael Latham

THE WORLD BANK
Washington, D.C.

ISBN: 978-0-8213-8249-3
eISBN: 978-0-8213-8333-9
DOI: 10.1596/978-0-8213-8249-3

Library of Congress Cataloging-in-Publication Data has been applied for.

Cover photos from istockphoto.com: Justice scale and gavel/DNY59/MBPHOTO, Inc.;
World War veteran with medals/a_Taigal; European currency/imagestock; dollars/
Mosich; scrolled stone column/Guy Sargent

Cover design: Critical Stages

Contents

Acknowledgments

This policy paper on politically exposed persons (PEPs) is the result of special collaborative efforts from colleagues around the world, whose time and expertise in the anti-money laundering field were generously shared. We especially thank the regulatory and bank officials as well as the financial intelligence units and law enforcement authorities with whom we met in Argentina; France; Hong Kong, China; Jersey; Liechtenstein; Switzerland; the United Kingdom; and the United States during our field visits.

This publication was written by Theodore S. Greenberg (Financial Market Integrity Unit, World Bank and PEP Team Leader) and Larissa Gray (Financial Market Integrity Unit, World Bank) with contributions from Delphine Schantz (Global Programme against Money Laundering Proceeds of Crime and the Financing of Terrorism, Law Enforcement, Organized Crime and Anti-Money Laundering Unit, UNODC), Nina Gidwaney (Financial Market Integrity Unit, World Bank), and Michael Latham and Carolin Gardner (UK Financial Services Authority, Financial Crime and Intelligence Division). A special thanks to Larissa Gray for her indefatigable work and support.

The PEP team is especially grateful to Jean Pesme (Manager, Financial and Private Sector Development) for his support and guidance on this project, and to Adrian Fozzard (StAR Coordinator) and James London (UK Financial Services Authority) for their guidance and suggestions.

The PEP team benefited from the insightful comments and discussion that helped shape the paper during the peer review. The peer reviewers were Elise Bean (Staff Director and Chief Counsel, United States Senate, Permanent Subcommittee on Investigations), André Corterier (Bundesanstalt für Finanzdienstleistungsaufsicht), Anthea Lawson and Robert Palmer (Global Witness), Samuel Munzele Maimbo (Senior Financial Sector Specialist, World Bank), Rick McDonell (Executive Secretary, Financial Action Task Force), Joseph Myers (Assistant General Counsel, Legal Department, International Monetary Fund), and Daniel Thelesklaf (Co-Director, International Centre for Asset Recovery). The team also benefited from the comments on the draft paper which were provided by many with whom we met during the field missions.

The team is grateful for the help provided by Pierre-Laurent Chatain (Financial Market Integrity Unit) and Ian Matthews (UK Financial Services Authority); and the involvement of Ruxandra Burdescu (Public Sector Governance, World Bank) and Elena Gasol Ramos (Transparency and Accountability, World Bank).

A special thanks to Miguel Nicolas de la Riva, Bjarne Hansen, and Maria Orellano (Financial Market Integrity Unit) and Kelley MacNab (UK Financial Services Authority) for their support.

Theodore S. Greenberg
PEP Team Leader (FPDFI)
World Bank

For further information, please contact:
Theodore S. Greenberg (tgreenberg@worldbank.org)
Larissa Gray (lgray@worldbank.org)

Abbreviations

AML	anti-money laundering
AML/CFT	anti-money laundering and combating the financing of terrorism
CDD	customer due diligence
DNFBPs	designated nonfinancial businesses and professions
EDD	enhanced due diligence
EU	European Union
FATF	Financial Action Task Force on Money Laundering
FATF 40+9	FATF Forty Recommendations on Money Laundering and Nine Special Recommendations on Terrorist Financing
FIU	financial intelligence unit
FSRB	FATF-Style Regional Body
G20	Group of twenty finance ministers and central bank governors (Argentina, Australia, Brazil, Canada, China, European Union, France, Germany, India, Indonesia, Italy, Japan, Mexico, the Russian Federation, Saudi Arabia, South Africa, the Republic of Korea, Turkey, the United Kingdom, and the United States)
GDP	gross domestic product
IMF	International Monetary Fund
KYC	know your customer
PEP	politically exposed person
StAR	World Bank/UNODC Stolen Asset Recovery Initiative
STR	suspicious transaction report
Third EU Directive	Collectively, Directive 2005/60/EC of the European Parliament and of the Council of October 26, 2005, on the prevention of the use of the financial system for the purpose of money laundering and terrorist financing; Commission Directive 2006/70/EC of August 1, 2006, laying down implementing measures for Directive 2005/60/EC with regard to the definition of "politically exposed person" and the technical criteria for simplified customer due diligence procedures and for exemption on grounds of a financial activity conducted on an occasional or very limited basis
UNCAC	United Nations Convention against Corruption
UNODC	United Nations Office on Drugs and Crime

Executive Summary and Principal Recommendations

Over the past 25 years, the whole world has learned about the gross abuses of corrupt "politically exposed persons" (PEPs), and through outrageous examples, the way in which they plunder state assets, extort and accept bribes, and use domestic and international financial systems to launder their stolen assets. In this paper PEPs include individuals who are, or have been, entrusted with prominent public functions and their family members and close associates.

We do not know the amount of public assets stolen or extorted by prominent public office holders—referred to as *grand corruption*—and mostly laundered through financial institutions, in particular, through banks. Attempts to estimate the sums of money being laundered are hindered by the fact that it is a mostly hidden crime for which accurate statistics are unavailable. At the same time, the "guesstimates" available on overall corruption and bribery offenses help to give an idea of the order of magnitude: The World Bank estimates that more than $1 trillion is paid in bribes each year.[1] The proceeds of corruption stolen from developing countries alone ranges from $20 billion to $40 billion per year—roughly equivalent to the annual GDP of the world's 12 poorest countries where more than 240 million people live.[2]

Grand corruption, asset theft, and international flows of stolen and laundered money have an insidious and devastating impact on development. They degrade and undermine confidence in public institutions. They taint and destabilize financial systems, affecting trust. They damage the victim country's investment climate and prospects for macroeconomic stability. This fuels capital flight, impedes growth and poverty reduction efforts, and heightens inequalities. These damages are long-lasting and become more severe the longer a corrupt regime is in place.[3] In all jurisdictions, political will at the highest levels is critical to fighting corruption and denying corrupt PEPs access to the financial system.

The ways in which corrupt PEPs launder their ill-gotten gains repeat and evolve. In the beginning, corrupt heads of state and prominent public officials banked in their

---

1. World Bank, "The Costs of Corruption," (April 8, 2004) quoting Daniel Kaufmann, Director for Governance, World Bank Institute. Link available at http://go.worldbank.org/LJA29GHA80.
2. UNODC and World Bank, "Stolen Asset Recovery (StAR) Initiative: Challenges, Opportunities, and Action Plan" (World Bank, Washington, DC, 2007), p. 9.
3. UNODC and World Bank, "Stolen Asset Recovery (StAR) Initiative: Challenges, Opportunities, and Action Plan" (World Bank, Washington, DC, 2007), p. 9.

own names in foreign jurisdictions or used relatives to open bank accounts. Current techniques continue to include abuse of bank facilities, but also the buying of real estate; the purchase and movement abroad of precious metals, jewels, and art work; and the physical cross-border movement of currency and negotiable instruments.[4] The use of close associates and corporate vehicles has been and remains a vexing problem. Ultimately most of the methods involve, at least in some way, the use of financial institutions, particularly banks, in the laundering of ill-gotten funds.

In addition to the early efforts of some governments, the international community made valuable commitments to address these pressing challenges. The United Nations Convention against Corruption was concluded in 2003. The same year, the Financial Action Task Force on Money Laundering (FATF) reviewed its Forty Recommendations to include standards that specifically target the laundering of the proceeds of corruption. We applaud those efforts and welcome the steps taken by several public agencies (including investigative and prosecutorial agencies), regulatory authorities, and banks to translate these commitments into practice. The reality, however, is that the distance between international commitment and visible effective action and impact remains wide. Steps taken have not been commensurate with the size and urgency of the challenge.

The Basel Committee on Banking Supervision, an international body of banking supervisors that formulates broad supervisory standards and guidance for implementation by its members, made plain the drawbacks of insufficient action for the international financial system as early as 2001:

> [I]t is clearly undesirable, unethical and incompatible with the fit and proper conduct of banking operations to accept or maintain a business relationship if the bank knows or must assume that the funds derive from corruption or misuse of public assets. There is a compelling need for a bank considering a relationship with a person whom it suspects of being a PEP to identify that person fully, as well as people and companies that are clearly related to him/her.[5]

> Accepting and managing funds from corrupt PEPs will severely damage the bank's own reputation and can undermine public confidence in the ethical standards of an entire financial centre, since such cases usually receive extensive media attention and strong political reaction.[6]

---

4. Money laundering is not confined to the financial services sector. The FATF 40+9 Recommendations apply to other sectors, referred to as designated nonfinancial businesses and professions (DNFBPs).

5. Basel Committee on Banking Supervision, "Customer Due Diligence for Banks," (Bank for International Settlements, October 2001), para. 43.

6. Basel Committee on Banking Supervision, "Customer Due Diligence for Banks," (Bank for International Settlements, October 2001), para. 42.

What is the reality? The picture today is of an overall failure of effective implementation of international PEP standards. There is surprisingly low compliance with FATF requirements on PEPs, especially among FATF members. Of the 124 countries assessed by FATF or by FATF-Style Regional Bodies, 61 percent were noncompliant and 23 percent were partially compliant. More than 80 percent of these jurisdictions are far behind.

This paper identifies three key actions necessary to make a genuine difference:

1. *Strong and sustained political will and mobilization.* Political will is needed to change laws and regulations, to create momentum for government authorities to make this a real priority, to ensure allocation of adequate resources, and to support more aggressive enforcement by regulators. Political will is also important on the implementation side: Absent such political commitment, some banks will not be motivated to make a meaningful commitment to improving customer due-diligence procedures with a view to detecting the proceeds of corruption.

2. *Clarification and harmonization of the international requirements on PEPs.* The current variations among approaches serve as both a good excuse not to act and are seen by some as a real impediment to the development and implementation of effective PEP controls. Harmonization would pave the way for useful guidance to be issued at the international or national level. Jurisdictions and banks would be provided with sounder and more consistent parameters.

3. *Stock-taking of the emerging typologies, with a focus on lifting what impedes the identification of beneficial owners who are PEPs.* PEP identification efforts are complicated by the increased use of close associates, legal entities, and other methods used to hide beneficial ownership or control by senior public officials.

Against this background, this StAR paper offers a series of recommendations and good practices designed to help increase the quality and effectiveness of those PEP measures adopted by regulatory authorities and banks. In addition, the paper provides recommendations that we hope the standard setters will consider.

Outlined below are the principal recommendations.

Principal Recommendation 1

Apply Enhanced Due Diligence to all PEPs, Foreign and Domestic

Laws and regulations should make no distinction between domestic and foreign PEPs. The standards adopted by FATF and regional and national standard setters should require similar enhanced due diligence for both foreign and domestic PEPs. The distinction between foreign and domestic PEPs in existing standards lets prominent domestic public officials and their families and close associates "off the hook." There is no justifiable basis for the distinction. All PEPs are exposed to the opportunity to misuse their position for personal gain; therefore, this distinction omits an important risk area. Most international banks already apply enhanced due diligence to both domestic and foreign PEPs, even though they are not required by law or regulation, and small banks generally are well aware of the identity of domestic PEPs. Thus little, if any, additional burden would be placed on banks applying this standard.

Principal Recommendation 2

Require a Declaration of Beneficial Ownership

At account opening and as needed thereafter, banks should require customers to complete a written declaration of the identity and details of the natural person(s) who are the ultimate beneficial owner(s) of the business relationship or transaction as a first step in meeting their beneficial ownership customer due diligence requirements (see the sample form in box 2.2). A critical problem identified by banks, regulators, and law enforcement alike is the recurring and intractable problem of untying the knot of legal entities formed for the purpose of hiding the identity of the natural persons who are the beneficial owners. Requiring a written declaration of beneficial ownership by the contracting customer should be an important first step in the bank's effort to identify and verify the identity of the beneficial owner. It is not the only step, nor is it sufficient on its own—banks must take additional measures to verify the declaration and conduct complementary customer due diligence, and regulatory authorities must ensure that additional actions are taken. The declaration is to be executed in a manner that provides for a criminal penalty for intentionally making a material false statement. While some criminals are unlikely to be deterred, officials and their family members and close associates will be less inclined to lie to banks if they face individual criminal liability for the false statement. In addition, the signed declaration could be used as evidence of criminal intent in a money laundering or fraud prosecution; the basis for a civil suit by the financial institution; a reason for closing the account; and an important piece of evidence in a nonconviction, based on a freezing or forfeiture proceeding initiated by the government.

Principal Recommendation 3

Request Asset and Income Disclosure Forms

A public official should be asked to provide a copy of any asset and income declaration forms filed with their authorities, as well as subsequent updates. If a customer refuses, the bank should assess the reasons and determine, using a risk-based approach, whether to proceed with the business relationship. More than 110 countries require that their public officials file asset and income disclosure forms. In the course of our research, we found only one bank that asks customers for a copy of the form, although all banks agreed that it was an additional tool and noted that they ask for the same information and more during account opening. The form provides an important "snapshot in time" that the bank can use to compare to information provided by the customer or with account activity. Because there may be legitimate reasons for the customer to decline to provide a copy or for not having filed the forms, the bank should ask about the reason for refusal and determine, using a risk-based approach, whether to open the account or continue the relationship. Verification by local authorities of the information on such forms is uneven across jurisdictions, so banks should remain cautious about the information provided, but it can help in customer profiling.

Principal Recommendation 4

Periodic Review of PEP Customers

PEP customers should be reviewed by senior management or a committee including at least one senior manager using a risk-based approach, at least yearly, and the results of the review should be documented. Over the course of a business relationship with a PEP, ongoing monitoring procedures may reveal changes to the profile and activity. The PEP may have been promoted or elected to a more senior position, engaged in litigation, or perhaps transactions have deviated from the norm. Considered separately, the activities, transactions, or profile changes may not be sufficient to raise "red flags." Once the information is assembled however, the "big picture" may reveal increases in overall risk or suspicions of corrupt activity. Implementing a periodic review of PEP customers using a risk-based approach, at least yearly, helps to create an overall view of a customer and overcome a narrow approach in which decisions are made transaction by transaction. This review is a common practice among the banks visited, and it ensures that the banks assemble a comprehensive picture of each PEP customer, which is analyzed and considered by senior management or a committee comprised of at least one senior manager on a regular basis. This enhances the oversight of the PEP by the bank's management. The individual or committee subsequently makes decisions on termination or continuation of the business relationship.

Principal Recommendation 5

Avoid Setting Limits on the Time a PEP Remains a PEP

Where a person has ceased to be entrusted with a prominent public function, countries should not introduce time limits on the length of time the person, family member, or close associate needs to be treated as a PEP. Many geographic, cultural, and political factors determine the duration of the power and influence held by public officials, relatives, and close associates. In many cases, the influence held by prominent public officials and close associates outlasts the term in office by years, even decades, and corrupt monies do not become legitimate after a certain time period. Rather than setting time limits, banks should be encouraged to consider the ongoing PEP status of their customers on a case-by-case basis using a risk-based approach, and regulatory authorities should provide guidance about what this entails. If the risk is low, banks can consider declassifying the relationship, but only after carefully evaluating the continuation of anti-money laundering risks and with the approval of senior management.

PART 1

Introduction and General Observations

1. Introduction

"Your doors are open to all sorts and conditions of men, except that you draw the line at dishonesty. You will not open even a deposit account with a stranger, unless he be satisfactorily introduced, lest you find that you have been entertaining a rascal unawares, who is making use of the cheque-book which you have supplied him with, to victimize half a score of innocent people."

George Rae, *The Country Banker: His Clients, Cares, and Work from an Experience of Forty Years,* (New York: Charles Scribner's Sons, 1886).

Revelations of grand corruption,[7] the scale of the plunder of state assets, and their impact on the confidence in financial institutions have led to greater scrutiny of business relationships with politically exposed persons (PEPs) with a view to addressing potential corruption and money laundering risks associated with these customers. PEPs—individuals who are, or have been, entrusted with prominent public functions and their family members and close associates—represent a greater money laundering risk because of the possibility that such individuals may abuse their position and influence to carry out corrupt acts, such as accept and extort bribes, misappropriate state assets, and then use domestic and international financial systems to launder the proceeds.[8] Obviously, most PEPs do not actually engage in corrupt activities; however, all PEPs are potentially in a position to misuse their positions for personal gain—no matter their country of origin, nature of business activities, or seniority of position.

While corrupt PEPs may be a small portion of the entire number of PEPs, a single corrupt PEP's behavior can have a disproportionate impact on a country and sometimes an entire region. Quantifying the amount of money that has been stolen and laundered

---

7. The term "corruption" is meant to include the offenses outlined in Articles 15-22 of UNCAC: Active bribery of national public officials; passive bribery of national public officials; active bribery of foreign public officials and officials of public international organisations; passive bribery of foreign public officials and officials of public international organizations; embezzlement, misappropriation, or other diversion of a property by a public official; trading in influence; abuse of functions or position by a public official for unlawful gain; illicit enrichment by a public official; bribery in the private sector; and embezzlement of property in the private sector. StAR considers there should be an alignment of the definitions of corruption with UNCAC, to be reflected in other StAR policy papers.
8. For the purposes of this paper, PEPs are to include individuals who are, or have been, entrusted with prominent public functions and their family members and close associates. For more information on the definition, see "Who Is a PEP?" in part 2 and the comparison chart in appendix C.

by corrupt PEPs has proven difficult.[9] The estimates available, therefore, provide rough approximations of the order of magnitude. The World Bank estimates that more than $1 trillion dollars is paid in bribes each year.[10] Furthermore, the Stolen Asset Recovery (StAR) Initiative has estimated that corrupt money received by public officials in developing and transition countries reaches $20 billion to $40 billion per year—a figure equivalent to 20 to 40 percent of flows of official development assistance.[11]

This scale of corruption leads to degradation and distrust of public institutions, insufficient government revenues, weakening of the private investment climate, and disruption of social service delivery mechanisms. The flows of dirty money damage the reputations of financial institutions and undermine public confidence in the integrity of the financial system. Implementation of an effective PEP regime is a critical component in the prevention of grand corruption because laundering the proceeds becomes more difficult. An effective PEP regime also assists in the detection of transfers of proceeds of corruption, provides an audit trail, and, ultimately, facilitates the process of recovering these proceeds.

In "Customer Due Diligence for Banks," a 2001 paper of the Basel Committee on Banking Supervision, the concept of PEPs was introduced by banking supervisors as a special category of individuals who expose a bank to significant reputation and legal risks.[12] The paper recognized the importance of providing guidance on the prudential risk posed by PEPs, stating "it is clearly undesirable, unethical and incompatible with the fit and proper conduct of banking operations to accept or maintain a business relationship if the bank knows or must assume that the funds derive from corruption or misuse of public assets."[13]

Eventually, the international community launched efforts to mitigate the potential risks posed by PEPs. In 2003, the Financial Action Task Force on Money Laundering (FATF) introduced a number of preventive measures to identify these higher risk individuals and to improve the monitoring of their transactions. These measures are set forth in Recommendation 6 of the FATF 40+9 Recommendations, with the related

9. UNODC and World Bank, "Stolen Asset Recovery (StAR) Initiative: Challenges, Opportunities, and Action Plan" (World Bank, Washington, DC, 2007) p. 9.
10. World Bank, "The Costs of Corruption," (April 8, 2004) quoting Daniel Kaufmann, Director for Governance, World Bank Institute. Link available at http://go.worldbank.org/LJA29GHA80.
11. UNODC and World Bank, "Stolen Asset Recovery (StAR) Initiative: Challenges, Opportunities, and Action Plan" (World Bank, Washington, DC, 2007) p. 9. At page 11, the report measures the development impact that could result from recovery of a portion of these assets. For example, every $100 million recovered could fund 3.3 million to 10 million insecticide-treated bednets or first-line treatment for over 600,000 people for one year for HIV/AIDS, or 250,000 water connections for households, or 240 kilometers of two-lane paved roads.
12. Basel Committee on Banking Supervision, "Customer Due Diligence for Banks," (Bank for International Settlements, October 2001), paras. 40-44.
13. Basel Committee on Banking Supervision, "Customer Due Diligence for Banks," (Bank for International Settlements, October 2001), para. 43.

requirements of customer due diligence in Recommendation 5. Also in 2003, the United Nations Convention against Corruption (UNCAC) called for enhanced scrutiny of accounts held by PEPs in Article 52(1) and (2) as a means to prevent and detect the transfer of the proceeds of crime. In 2006, FATF stated that the lack of rule of law and measures to prevent and combat corruption may significantly impair the implementation of an effective anti-money laundering/combating the financing of terrorism framework.[14] In addition, studies have been undertaken by FATF and the FATF-Style Regional Bodies (FSRBs) on PEPs in the context of corruption and money laundering.[15]

Anti-money laundering (AML) regimes, particularly the PEP provisions, vary in scope across the standard setters.[16] All require countries to ensure that financial institutions consider PEPs to be high-risk customers and, accordingly, implement systems for their identification, with enhanced due diligence procedures at account opening, and ongoing monitoring and reporting of suspicious transactions. Below is the relevant text of the United Nations Convention against Corruption (UNCAC) and the FATF 40+9 Recommendations. See appendix C for comparative tables of the definitions and enhanced due diligence requirements provided in international standards and European Union legislation.

Article 52 of UNCAC:

1. [...] each State Party shall take such measures as may be necessary, in accordance with its domestic law, to require banks within its jurisdiction to verify the identity of customers, to take reasonable steps to determine the identity of beneficial owners of funds deposited into high-value accounts and to ***conduct enhanced scrutiny of accounts sought or maintained by or on behalf of individuals who are, or have been, entrusted with prominent public functions and their family members and associates.*** Such enhanced scrutiny shall be reasonably designed to detect suspicious transactions for the purpose of reporting to competent authorities and should not be so construed as to discourage or prohibit banks from doing business with any legitimate customer. [***emphasis added***]

---

14. FATF Methodology, Introduction, para. 7.

15. FATF/APG (Asia Pacific Group on Money-Laundering) Project Group on Corruption and Money Laundering has also conducted research on PEPs: Dr. David Chaikin and Dr. Jason Sharman, "FATF/APG Anti-Corruption AML/CFT Research Paper," (September 2007). See also APG Annual Meeting, "IIWG Implementation Issues Report: Corruption-Related FATF Recommendations 2009"; "Politically Exposed Persons (PEPs) in relation to AML/CFT," (Middle East & North Africa Financial Action Task Force, November 11, 2008); Kwesi Aning & Samuel Atuobi, "The Nexus Between Corruption and Money Laundering in West Africa: the Case of Ghana," draft to be presented to GIABA (Inter Governmental Action Group Against Money Laundering in West Africa) in 2009; and "An Assessment of the Links between Corruption and the Implementation of Anti-Money Laundering Strategies and Measures in the ESAAMLG Region," (Eastern and Southern Africa Anti-Money Laundering Group [ESAAMLG], May 18, 2009).

16. Unless otherwise specified, this paper uses the term "standard setters" broadly to include the standards outlined in the FATF 40+9 Recommendations, international instruments (UNCAC), and national or regional legislative acts.

2. […] In order to facilitate implementation of the measures provided for in paragraph 1 of this article, each State Party, in accordance with its domestic law and inspired by relevant initiatives of regional, interregional and multilateral organizations against money laundering, shall:

(a) Issue advisories regarding the types of natural or legal person to whose accounts banks within its jurisdiction will be expected to apply enhanced scrutiny, the types of accounts and transactions to which to pay particular attention and appropriate account-opening, maintenance and recordkeeping measures to take concerning such accounts; and

(b) Where appropriate, notify banks within its jurisdiction, at the request of another State Party or on its own initiative, of the identity of particular natural or legal persons to whose accounts such institutions will be expected to apply enhanced scrutiny, in addition to those whom the banks may otherwise identify.

Recommendation 6 of the FATF 40 Recommendations: Banks should, in relation to politically exposed persons, in addition to performing normal due diligence measures:

a) Have appropriate risk management systems to determine whether the customer is a politically exposed person.

b) Obtain senior management approval for establishing business relationships with such customers.

c) Take reasonable measures to establish the source of wealth and source of funds.

d) Conduct enhanced ongoing monitoring of the business relationship.

FATF "Glossary of Definitions used in the Methodology" defines PEPs as "individuals who are or have been entrusted with prominent public functions in a foreign country, for example Heads of State or of government, senior politicians, senior government, judicial or military officials, senior executives of state owned corporations, important political party officials. Business relationships with family members or close associates of PEPs involve reputational risks similar to those with PEPs themselves. The definition is not intended to cover middle ranking or more junior individuals in the foregoing categories."

In March 2009, the Group of 20 (G20) countries called for enforcement of these standards on PEPs as a means to deter corruption and detect and deter the flow of proceeds of corruption in its "Working Group on Reinforcing International Cooperation and Promoting Integrity in Financial Markets."[17] In September 2009, the G20 Heads of

---

17. G20 Working Group on Reinforcing International Cooperation and Promoting Integrity in Financial Markets (WG2), "Final Report," March 27, 2009, para. 41.

State called for the ratification of UNCAC and asked FATF to focus on detecting and deterring the proceeds of corruption by strengthening standards on customer due diligence, beneficial ownership, and transparency.[18] FATF will be considering these issues as part of the preparation for the fourth round of mutual evaluations.

Industry groups, such as the Wolfsberg Group, have issued guidance papers and recommendations.[19] The private sector has responded with products to assist banks in identifying PEPs, such as commercial PEP databases and software that mines data for the key information required to assess the relevant risks.

Low Compliance with International Standards

With UNCAC ratified by 141 countries and the FATF Recommendations adopted as the AML standard by more than 170 jurisdictions, most jurisdictions in the world have committed to meaningful and effective action. However, according to the latest round of FATF and FSRB mutual evaluation reports, more than 80 percent of jurisdictions so far have not translated this commitment into effective measures. Of the 124 jurisdictions that have been evaluated for compliance with FATF Recommendation 6, 61 percent were found noncompliant and 23 percent were partially compliant. Only three jurisdictions were found to be fully compliant. These trends are observed in FATF and FSRB jurisdictions alike, with compliance levels lower in FATF jurisdictions. See figures 1.1 and 1.2.

Figure 1.1 FATF Recommendation 6: Compliance of 124 Jurisdictions

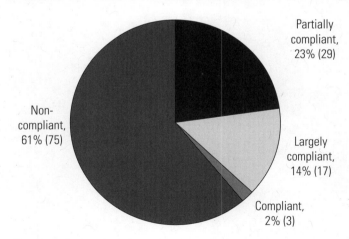

Source: Authors' compilation based upon the compliance ratings published in the FATF and the FSRB mutual evaluation reports of 124 jurisdictions.
Note: Numbers in parentheses refer to the number of jurisdictions.

18. G20, "Leaders' Statement, The Pittsburgh Summit," (September 24-25, 2009).
19. The Wolfsberg Group, an association of 11 global banks, has developed a series of financial industry standards in relation to anti-money laundering and released specific information concerning PEPs.

Figure 1.2 FATF Recommendation 6: FATF and Non-FATF Country Ratings

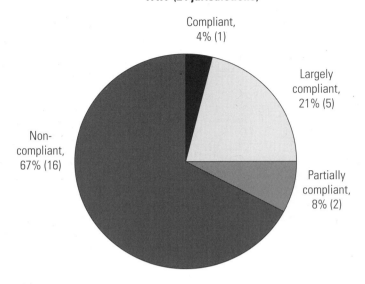

FATF (24 jurisdictions)

Compliant, 4% (1)

Largely compliant, 21% (5)

Partially compliant, 8% (2)

Non-compliant, 67% (16)

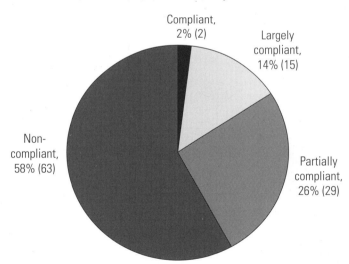

FSRBs (Non-FATF) (109 jurisdictions)

Compliant, 2% (2)

Largely compliant, 14% (15)

Partially compliant, 26% (29)

Non-compliant, 58% (63)

Source: Authors' compilation based upon the compliance ratings published in the FATF and the FSRB mutual evaluation reports of 124 jurisdictions.

Note: Numbers in parentheses refer to the number of jurisdictions. As some jurisdictions are members of both the FATF and an FSRB, there is overlap in these numbers.

Objective

This policy paper has been undertaken by the Stolen Asset Recovery Initiative, a joint initiative of the United Nations Office on Drugs and Crime and the World Bank. Given the lack of compliance with international standards on PEPs, StAR launched this policy paper to assist banks and regulatory authorities in building regimes that will help address the risks posed by PEPs and prevent corrupt PEPs from abusing domestic and international financial systems to launder the proceeds of corruption.[20]

This paper offers a series of Recommendations and Good Practices designed to help increase the quality and effectiveness of PEP measures of regulatory authorities and banks. In addition, the paper provides Recommendations that we hope the standard setters and policy makers might consider in strengthening the existing PEP regimes.

Methodology

The main research for this paper was based on field work conducted in eight jurisdictions with experience in dealing with PEPs.[21] The jurisdictions represent different regions and regulatory frameworks. Additional research was conducted in seven jurisdictions,[22] as well as the relevant portions of 82 FATF and FSRB mutual evaluation reports filed in the third round of evaluations.[23] The adoption of the mutual evaluation reports began after a reasonable period of time following the issuance of the revised FATF 40+9 Recommendations in 2003 (the first assessment was adopted in mid-2005) and have been ongoing. These reports represent a "snapshot" of the situation in the respective country at the date of the assessment. Some countries may have progressed in terms of compliance since the assessment.

The purpose of the field work was not to assess or rate jurisdictions, but rather to obtain an overview and learn from authorities and the private sector about the policies and practices in implementing compliance with international PEP standards and some of the common obstacles to the effective application of PEP measures. The examples used throughout the paper, therefore, are not attributed to any particular jurisdiction.

---

20. The objective of the StAR Initiative is to reduce barriers to asset recovery and thereby encourage and facilitate more systematic and timely return of stolen assets. For more information on the StAR Initiative see www.worldbank.org/star.

21. Argentina; France; Hong Kong, China; Jersey; Liechtenstein; Switzerland; the United Kingdom; and the United States.

22. Lebanon, Mexico, Nigeria, the Russian Federation, Singapore, South Africa, and the United Arab Emirates.

23. Jurisdictions selected were those in the previously listed 15 jurisdictions, as well as jurisdictions that have a publicly available FATF or FSRB mutual evaluation report available in English and published after June 2007.

A list of interview questions was designed to serve as a basis for discussion and to ensure that a consistent and transparent method for collecting information during the field work was followed.[24] During the field visits, members of the team met with a number of authorities, including regulators (independent or within the central bank), financial intelligence units (FIUs), law enforcement, and where appropriate the public prosecutor. Members of the team also met with senior officials of two banks in each jurisdiction.[25] Throughout the course of writing the paper, the team met with three commercial database companies or platform providers. In advance of publication, a copy of this policy paper was circulated to these authorities and bank officials and they were invited to comment.

How to Use This Paper

This paper is designed as a policy note for banks and regulatory authorities, as well as for use by the standard setters, policy makers, FIUs, and other public authorities with a role in the implementation of PEP standards. The Recommendations and Good Practices included in the paper should therefore be reviewed and considered by each of these stakeholders. Banks may use a Recommendation or Good Practice to improve the quality and effectiveness of their PEP measures; regulatory authorities may use them to enhance their review and enforcement processes on PEPs; and regulatory authorities, financial intelligence units, and other public authorities may use them to develop or improve guidance. Similarly, policy makers and standard setters may use the Recommendations and Good Practices to inform their efforts in ensuring that effective laws and standards are adopted.

The paper is focused on the banking sector, not on other financial and nonfinancial sectors vulnerable to the laundering of corrupt funds.[26] These other sectors may find the Recommendations and Good Practices provided in this paper relevant, but should analyze the findings of this paper in light of their particular circumstances and specific features.

The paper includes a number of practical tools to help guide banks, regulators, and other public authorities. These tools are illustrative, not exhaustive, and therefore should not in any way be relied upon as a comprehensive source, but rather as a starting point.

---

24. The questionnaire addressed issues of the implementation by various national entities of PEP systems and procedures, as well as the regulatory and enforcement aspects. Written answers were not expected, although some were provided. For a copy of the questionnaire, see appendix G.

25. In one jurisdiction, the team met with one bank. In most cases, these institutions were part of larger international banking groups with sophisticated AML systems and controls and risks of high-level PEP exposure.

26. While it would be helpful to understand what is happening across the various sectors on PEPs, such a detailed analysis was beyond the scope of this policy paper.

The paper is organized into four major parts:

The remainder of this part (part 1) sets out some of the main observations and trends in PEPs compliance and an analysis of the principal reasons for poor compliance and overall ineffectiveness of systems to detect and monitor PEPs. Part 2 focuses on the implementation of PEP measures by regulatory authorities and banks. Part 3 reviews the roles of the public authorities that are primarily involved in preventing abuse by corrupt PEPs. These authorities include the regulatory authority, which is responsible for providing guidance to banks and enforcing compliance, as well as the FIU, which has a role in the context of suspicious transaction reports (STRs) on PEPs. Finally, Part 4 considers some of the cross-cutting issues—national cooperation, training, and resources—that must be addressed by all stakeholders.

2. General Observations and Challenges

This chapter sets out some of the main observations and trends in PEP compliance and an analysis of the principal reasons for poor compliance and overall ineffectiveness of systems to detect and monitor PEPs.

Low Level of Compliance with International Standards

As indicated in the previous chapter, compliance with FATF Recommendation 6 is poor.[27] The low levels of compliance are not concentrated in certain regions; nor are compliance rates better in the more developed jurisdictions. On the contrary, compliance rates are relatively worse in developed countries. Similar trends of noncompliance are observed across jurisdictions of FATF and FSRBs. See figure 1.3.

A key factor in these low ratings is the lack of an enforceable legal or regulatory framework. The team's review of 82 mutual evaluation reports from FATF and the FSRBs found that, at the time of the evaluation, 40 percent of the jurisdictions did not have enforceable legislation or regulations concerning PEPs.[28] Where PEP-specific legal provisions, regulations, or other enforceable guidance existed, they were often not applied to all sectors within the scope of the FATF 40+9 Recommendations. Information on the effectiveness of actual implementation was limited. In addition, some of the existing laws have a narrow definition of enhanced due diligence (for example, a number of countries only required senior management approval for *new* PEP customers identified during account opening, not for *existing* customers who became a PEP.)

Link between PEPs and Anti-Money Laundering Policies and Procedures

PEPs are a special category of customer, all designated as high risk for money laundering. This designation is set out in the FATF 40+9 Recommendations, which introduce

---

27. Of 124 jurisdictions, 61 percent were noncompliant, 23 percent were partially compliant, 14 percent were largely compliant and 2 percent were compliant.
28. See also the APG Corruption Implementation Issues Report which also notes the lack of legislative, regulatory, or other enforceable means on PEPs: APG Annual Meeting, "IIWG Implementation Issues Report: Corruption-Related FATF Recommendations," 2009.

Figure 1.3 Ratings Summary of FATF Recommendation 6

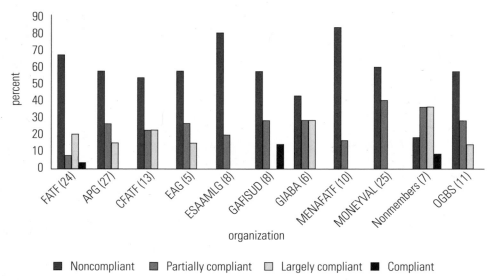

■ Noncompliant   ■ Partially compliant   □ Largely compliant   ■ Compliant

Source: Authors' compilation based upon the compliance ratings published in the FATF and the FSRB mutual evaluation reports of 124 jurisdictions.

Note: Numbers in parentheses refer to the number of jurisdictions. As some jurisdictions are members of both FATF and one or more FSRB, there is overlap in these numbers.

APG = Asia/Pacific Group on Money Laundering; CFATF = Caribbean Financial Action Task Force; MONEYVAL = Committee of Experts on the Evaluation of Anti-Money Laundering Measures and the Financing of Terrorism; EAG = The Eurasian Group on Combating Money Laundering and Financing of Terrorism; ESAAMLG = Eastern and Southern Africa Anti-Money Laundering Group; FATF = Financial Action Task Force on Money Laundering; GAFISUD = Financial Action Task Force of South America Against Money Laundering; GIABA = The Inter-Governmental Action Group against Money Laundering in West Africa; MENAFATF = Middle East & North Africa Financial Action Task Force; OGBS = Offshore Group of Banking Supervisors.

PEPs as one of the three specific cases that are *always* considered to be a higher risk. PEPs should normally be identified in the course of a bank's customer due diligence (CDD) procedures (including identification of the beneficial owner), which forms an integral part of a bank's AML system and controls. Failures or lack of completeness of customer due diligence procedures (up to the identification of the beneficial owner) create a risk that a bank will not identify a PEP or misjudge the risks associated with a particular PEP customer. A bank's PEP controls will, therefore, only be as good as its overall AML framework.

This link is confirmed by a comparison between compliance ratings on FATF Recommendation 5 on CDD and Recommendation 6 on PEPs. Of the 124 jurisdictions evaluated for compliance, 93 percent of the jurisdictions were either noncompliant or partially compliant with Recommendation 5; 84 percent of the same 124 jurisdictions received the same ratings on Recommendation 6. Only 17 jurisdictions had a rating of partially compliant or noncompliant in one category and largely compliant or compliant in another. See figure 1.4.

Figure 1.4 Ratings Summary of Recommendations 5 and 6

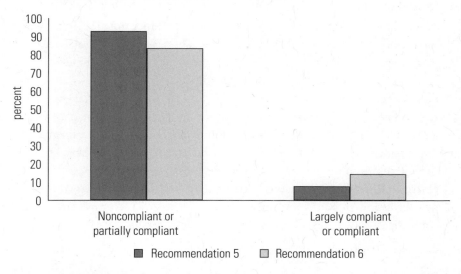

Source: Authors' compilation based upon the compliance ratings published in the FATF and the FSRB mutual evaluation reports of 124 jurisdictions.

Banks Generally Indicate Doing More Than FATF, Legislation, or Regulation Requires

Most of the banks visited indicated that they go beyond the legal definition of a PEP and apply a broader scope of enhanced due diligence (EDD) measures than those required under either domestic legislation or regulation. For example, some do not distinguish between domestic and foreign PEPs, even when they are only required by national law to apply EDD to foreign PEPs (for additional examples, see various chapters in part 2). This exacting policy is driven mainly by reputational risk considerations and group policies designed to comply with the most stringent requirements of the jurisdictions within which they operate. Some banks also cited concerns about possible legal or regulatory action.

In the jurisdictions visited as part of the fieldwork, banks and public authorities both explained that there is scant evidence of corrupt PEP activity—either within the banks or within the other sectors. Similarly, there are few PEP-related suspicious transaction reports or investigations and prosecutions for grand corruption. They indicated that this was because of several factors:

- Banks' are firmly resolved to accept only "clean" PEPs as customers. Banks indicated that they have improved their identification of PEPs and, as indicated above, often go beyond international standards, legislation, and regulation. The result is that PEPs of questionable integrity are refused access to banking services.

- The proportion of prominent public officials and their relatives in relation to a bank's overall customer base is likely to be small. Of the banks visited, the proportion of PEPs ranged from 1 percent to 5 percent.[29] Since not all PEPs are corrupt, those who are corrupt form an even smaller subset. Banks were not as clear on the percentage of close associates—in part because they are harder to identify.
- Corrupt PEPs are effectively hiding their identity from the banks, using associates and complex corporate vehicles to disguise their beneficial ownership of funds. They use intermediaries, such as accountants, lawyers, or trust and company service providers, who are involved on their behalf in the formation and management of corporate vehicles and schemes, but who may have little awareness of, or are complicit in, the unlawful conduct of the PEP.[30]
- Corrupt PEPs often seek the path of least resistance, placing the proceeds of corruption in banks and jurisdictions where AML controls are weak, less sophisticated, or good on paper but poorly enforced.

Why Focus on PEPs?

If, as banks report, the number of corrupt PEPs is so low, is it really worth the resources expended? The following are some of the key reasons why policy makers need to increase efforts on PEPs:

- Corruption has a devastating effect on development outcomes in some of the world's poorest countries. An individual corrupt PEP can have a disproportionate impact on a country or region.
- PEPs pose a substantial legal and reputational risk to the individual bank, and a reputational risk to a jurisdiction's financial sector as a whole. The PEP scandals experienced in the past 20 years involving heads of state, senior officials and their family members and close associates have clearly demonstrated that a bank's reputation will be very negatively affected and that public confidence in the ethical standards and even stability of the entire financial system can be undermined. Compliance levels with Recommendation 6 indicate insufficient mitigation of this risk.
- Standard CDD is not sufficient, as proven by previous scandals.
- Banks are already taking action on PEPs and many even go beyond the international standards. Providing clearer, more stringent legislation and regulations on PEPs may assist banks legally in putting more ambitious measures into place and, in practice, will "level the playing field" between banks.

---

29. During the field visits, some banks shared their total number of PEPs and related statistics on STR filings. Other banks shared a range (for example, "less than 10").

30. The FATF "Glossary of Definitions Used in the Methodology" states that "intermediaries can be financial institutions, designated nonfinancial businesses and professions (DNFBPs) or other reliable persons or businesses that meet Criteria 9.1 to 9.4." The same glossary states that DNFBPs include casinos, real estate agents, dealers in precious metals, dealers in precious stones, lawyers, notaries, other independent legal professionals and accountants, and trust and company service providers.

- Low numbers of PEP customers are not necessarily indicative of low numbers of corrupt PEPs. Instead—as the banks themselves suggested—corrupt PEPs are becoming more effective in hiding their identity through associates, legal and corporate entities, and intermediaries. Thus, greater attention and increased efforts in these areas will likely improve the identification and detection of corrupt PEPs.

The most pressing issue is how to make sense of the following conundrum: If, as the World Bank report suggests, $1 trillion of corruption money is moving around the world each year, where is it? There is also a sharp disconnect between what is happening in practice, as evidenced by actual corruption investigations (the true beneficial owner is not always identified) and what banks say they are doing (always determining the beneficial owners). Given the estimated scale of the funds involved, as well as clear indications that corrupt PEPs are using more sophisticated avenues to launder the proceeds of corruption and that there is poor compliance with international PEP standards, the money must be moving undetected through the banks and intermediaries and the current systems are failing to detect it.

Why Is PEP Compliance Such a Problem?

Many technical challenges have been discussed over recent years, with issues ranging from differences in the definition to difficulties associated with identifying a PEP who is the beneficial owner. Money laundering schemes are increasingly complex and opaque which makes the identification of a PEP increasingly difficult for everyone in the financial system. In addition, there is a practical difficulty in the international community identifying or demanding action, especially in countries with key natural resources or those who play important regional roles. Those who benefit from corruption create a powerful constituency that discourages identifying or monitoring of PEP accounts and may attempt to discredit or silence anticorruption organizations and leaders.

However, political will is, and will remain, a prerequisite for any PEP regime to be successful. The current lack of mobilization is reflected in the low priority accorded to the PEP issue or, in some cases, the failure to enact legislation or promulgate and implement regulations. This extends to the international realm, where standard setters set different standards and do not provide clear guidance, and standards lag behind those used by some key players in the private sector. This lack of a coherent approach subsequently impacts the implementation of PEP measures: Regulatory authorities have little incentive to enact regulatory requirements and enforce them; and without risk of enforcement action, some banks will risk playing the system (that is, a "race to the bottom"). Parts 2, 3, and 4 of this paper further analyze these issues and provide Recommendations and Good Practices to help reverse this trend.

1. *Lack of political mobilization.*

Without political will and resolve, public authorities have little incentive to allocate sufficient human and financial resources to improve or guide compliance with PEP standards. Nor will they aggressively enforce PEP requirements if they are unsure that their decisions will be supported by authorities. Of the jurisdictions visited, many public authorities had not publicly discussed the PEP issue beyond the mere application of international standards. More specifically,

- None of the jurisdictions visited cited examples of recent regulatory sanctions—an effective tool for generating improvements in the industry—for failure to comply with PEP requirements. Only one regulator had conducted a thematic review on the issue of PEPs (see the "Regulatory Authorities" chapter in part 3).
- Some jurisdictions exhibit an apparent lack of responsiveness from FIUs on PEP issues, evidenced by the general complaints from banks that not enough feedback or guidance is provided by FIUs on PEPs. (see the "Suspicious Transaction Reporting and Financial Intelligence Units" chapter in part 3).
- Very few authorities had considered measuring the effectiveness of PEP measures, for example through collection of statistics or other studies, whether by the regulatory authorities or FIUs.
- In one case, a bank's stringent PEP controls conflicted with the host country's strict data protection laws. Such tensions might be perfectly legitimate in themselves, but the absence of steps taken to resolve them (leaving the private sector to deal with them on a day-to-day basis) indicates a lack of commitment.

Although one government has established a series of groups that bring together key stakeholders—law enforcement, the regulator, prosecutors, and the private sector—to streamline its PEP efforts and increase effectiveness,[31] the overall lack of attention from public authorities means that banks have less incentive to allocate sufficient resources to earnestly identifying and mitigating PEP risks.

2. *Clarification and harmonization of the international requirements.*

International standard setters agree that a PEP is a natural person who is or has been entrusted with a prominent public function. Aside from this area of agreement, however, there is neither consistent terminology nor scope of the PEP definition and underlying requirements in the international standards, interpretative notes, and methodologies. This variability has led to confusion about the different definitions and requirements, as well as how to implement them. Some of the key differences, also outlined in table form in appendix C,[32] include the following:

---

31. For additional information on standing PEP groups, see the "National Cooperation: Agencies and the Industry" chapter in part 4.
32. Relevant provisions of UNCAC, FATF, and the Third EU Directive can also be found in appendixes D, E, and F, respectively.

- *Foreign versus domestic PEPs.* UNCAC calls for EDD for both foreign and domestic PEPs; FATF applies this requirement to foreign PEPs only, although an interpretative note "encourages" countries to extend the requirement to domestic PEPs (see also the "Who Is a PEP?" chapter in part 2).
- *Officials and their family members and close associates.* The wording in UNCAC includes family and associates more expressly than does the wording in the FATF 40+9 Recommendations. With regard to close associates, UNCAC defines them to include companies and natural persons, but FATF does not specify (see also the "Who Is a PEP?" in part 2).
- *Other categories:* There are a number of categories that are included in some definitions and excluded or limited in others (e.g., military officers, diplomats, judiciary) (see also the "Who Is a PEP?" in part 2).

Some jurisdictions have taken efforts to clarify the PEP definition by elaborating categories. One example is the Third Money Laundering Directive adopted by the European Union (Third EU Directive) and its implementing measures.[33] The Third EU Directive provides a specific legal PEP framework for European Union Member States. It is based upon the FATF definition and requirements, but differs in some core points (for example, rather than requiring EDD on all foreign PEPs as obliged under FATF, Article 13(4) of the Third EU Directive requires EDD only on PEPs *residing* in a foreign country). In an attempt to provide more guidance on the FATF definition, the implementing measures to the Third EU Directive lists examples of categories for PEPs. The implementing measures also introduce a one-year time period for those who have left office, after which the former prominent public official, their family members or close associates no longer need to be treated as a PEP. The measures narrow the scope of "family" to immediate families. These provisions have added further confusion to the definition issue for some banks and seem too narrow in light of typologies (see also the "Who Is a PEP?" chapter and the "How Long Is a PEP Considered a PEP" chapter in part 2).

3. *"The classic corrupt PEP is dead": Stock-taking of the emerging typologies, focused on lifting impediments to the identification of beneficial ownership.*

All parties visited advised, and anecdotal evidence suggests, that the classic methodology of corrupt PEPs putting funds directly into their own named accounts or that of immediate family members is apparently now a rarity. This could be read as a sign

---

33. Directive 2005/60/EC of the European Parliament and of the Council of October 26, 2005, on the prevention of the use of the financial system for the purpose of money laundering and terrorist financing; Commission Directive 2006/70/EC of August 1, 2006, laying down implementing measures for Directive 2005/60/EC with regard to the definition of "politically exposed person" and the technical criteria for simplified customer due diligence procedures and for exemption on grounds of a financial activity conducted on an occasional or very limited basis. For the text of the directives, see appendix F. Provisions have since been enshrined in domestic legislation in most of the Member States.

of success; however, banks and some law enforcement representatives also stated (and actual cases confirm) that corrupt PEPs are now increasingly using less known associates and more complex corporate and trust arrangements to veil the identity of the PEP or the PEP's beneficial ownership. The use of company formation agents and lawyers, accountants, and financial advisers to create and manage a PEP's affairs can further complicate bank identification of PEP beneficial owners. This difficulty is exacerbated if PEPs are based in jurisdictions with weak AML legislation, if the home jurisdiction of the PEP has limited access to public information or imposes restrictions on media reporting of information that could be relevant or if the jurisdiction where the PEP sets up a corporate vehicle does not require transparency over the beneficial ownership.

PART 2

Implementation of International
Standards on PEPs by Banks and
Regulatory Authorities

3. Applying a Risk-Based Approach

Many of the jurisdictions studied and visited apply a risk-based approach to anti-money laundering (AML). The application of a risk-based approach by countries, regulatory authorities, and the financial system has been outlined in the Financial Action Task Force on Money Laundering (FATF) "Guidance on the Risk-Based Approach to Combating Money Laundering and Terrorist Financing." This paper will not attempt to explain the risk-based approach in detail (see box 2.1 for an explanation of its application in banks).[34]

Setting aside the general application of a risk-based approach, how do banks, regulatory authorities, and jurisdictions use the risk-based approach in the context of politically exposed persons (PEPs)? Unfortunately, there is no simple answer. It is important to stress from the outset that a risk-based approach is to be applied throughout the process, from the core customer due diligence (CDD) measures to having appropriate risk management systems to identify and verify PEPs up to enhanced ongoing monitoring.[35] Once identified as such, a PEP has to be considered a high-risk customer. Essentially, there are two successive steps. First is customer identification and verification, which can follow a risk-based approach as the bank gathers information on its customer. Identification and verification measures are to include mechanisms to identify PEPs. Second is the ability to have gradation in the enhanced due diligence (EDD) inside the high-risk PEP category in order to take account of the real risk posed by each individual PEP customer. This paper attempts to highlight the practical application of such a risk-based approach in relevant chapters.

Although the banks visited as part of the fieldwork were well-versed in applying a risk-based approach, it was suggested that some banks were abusing its flexibility (for example, tailoring it to suit their business model rather than their risk model). These banks use the risk-based approach to apply PEP measures in a manner that does not account for all the risks, or resort to a box-checking approach.

---

34. FATF "Guidance on the Risk-Based Approach to Combating Money Laundering and Terrorist Financing" http://www.fatf-gafi.org/dataoecd/43/46/38960576.pdf.
35. FATF Recommendation 6(a) requires "appropriate risk management systems to determine whether the customer is a PEP."

> **BOX 2.1** **Applying a Risk-Based Approach in Banks**
>
> For banks, a risk-based approach to AML means focusing resources on where the greatest risks lie. A risk-based approach is an alternative to more prescriptive approaches in which requirements are similar irrespective of the customer's risk profile, and in which resources are spread evenly across different business areas independently of the AML risks, or focus on certain predetermined areas only. A risk-based approach assumes that a bank has performed a thorough analysis of the AML risks it faces, given its business profile, products, and the specifics of its customer base.
>
> Under a risk-based approach, a bank is responsible to identify the AML risks it faces, and use informed judgment to design the most appropriate policies and procedures to mitigate the risks identified. In this process, the bank will refer to information made available by public authorities to complement its own sources.
>
> If applied correctly, a risk-based approach presents the following advantages in addressing PEP risks:
>
> - **It is flexible.** PEP risk varies across customers, jurisdictions, products and delivery channels, and over time.
>
> - **It is effective.** Banks are well-placed to effectively assess and mitigate the particular PEP risks they face.
>
> - **It is proportionate.** The approach focuses resources on where the PEP risks lie.
>
> However, a poorly or partially applied risk-based approach will leave gaps in controls, thereby rendering the system vulnerable to abuse, and is likely to produce inferior results compared with those of more prescriptive alternatives. Using a risk-based approach is neither cheap nor easy, and presupposes, among other things, the existence of good and up-to-date information and intelligence, the availability of sufficient resources and technical expertise at the bank and the regulatory authority to assess this information, and adequate resources to mitigate the risks identified. A risk-based approach might, therefore, not be the best solution in jurisdictions or financial institutions where these conditions cannot be met.

Recommendations:

- Countries should carefully consider whether a risk-based approach will produce the best results. In doing so, they should consider the extent to which qualitative information that could inform risk assessments is readily available, the ability of the regulator to supervise and guide the sector, and the extent to which banks are equipped with sufficient resources and expertise to identify and mitigate any money laundering and PEP risks they face.

- Where a risk-based approach is applied, regulatory authorities need to make efforts to ensure that the entire sector understands the approach and is applying it correctly, including in the context of PEP systems and controls.

4. Who Is a PEP?

Identifying customers, such as PEPs, who pose an increased risk of laundering corrupt funds is an important part of a bank's AML controls. Essential to the identification process is having a definition of PEPs. Unfortunately, as outlined in "General Observations and Challenges" in part 1, there is no internationally agreed-upon definition of PEPs. As a result, understanding who these customers are and how far the definition of PEPs should stretch is a difficult and politically sensitive topic.

Standard setters generally agree that PEPs are individuals who are, or have been, entrusted with prominent public functions, such as heads of state or government.[36] The standard setters and a considerable number of jurisdictions also expect financial institutions to treat a prominent public official's family and close associates as PEPs.[37]

Attempts to provide increased clarity to the definition have resulted in some standard setters limiting the scope of the PEP definition to exclude domestic PEPs, family members beyond immediate family, and junior and middle-ranking PEPs. In some cases, countries have issued a limited list of positions that financial institutions are obliged to consider as politically exposed. Some of these restrictions may be designed to allow for greater efforts to be expended on more-exposed PEPs (limitations on junior and middle-ranking PEPs). Flexibility on this matter also seems to make sense for individual jurisdictions. At the same time, core definitions that are too restrictive (for example, including only immediate families and close associates) are likely to create loopholes—as evidenced by actual corruption cases.

Interestingly, most of the banks visited have developed a definition that extends to a broader group than required by the standard setters or by national law or regulation.

The adoption by FATF and the United Nations Convention against Corruption of a uniform, worldwide definition is overdue. Many of the stakeholders visited indicated that the lack of clarity in the international definitions is confusing and, more importantly, has frustrated implementation efforts. Anecdotal evidence suggests that the lack of a clear definition may also be used as an excuse for failing to take any efforts, whether by a jurisdiction, regulatory authority, or a bank. While this paper does not attempt to propose a definition, it does outline a number of core elements to be included, such as their applicability to both foreign and domestic prominent public officials, close associates, and family members (see

---

36. FATF Glossary; Article 52(1), UNCAC.
37. FATF Glossary; Article 52(1), UNCAC.

below for additional descriptions and other issues for consideration). A good definition will strike a balance between being comprehensive and being workable. It will be a guide rather than a set of inflexible rules, and will allow banks to focus their efforts on where the real risks lie. A helpful aid in reviewing this section is table A1.1 in appendix C.

Recommendation:

FATF and UNCAC should align the definition of PEPs. This definition should be adopted by national standard setters and other key stakeholders.

Domestic versus Foreign PEPs

The standard setters have not applied a consistent requirement on the issue of whether PEP standards apply to foreign or domestic PEPs, or both. The FATF 40+9 Recommendations apply the PEP provisions to foreign PEPs only, although an interpretive note encourages countries to extend the requirement to domestic PEPs.[38]

Conversely, UNCAC does not distinguish between foreign and domestic PEPs, which has the effect of requiring that States Parties mandate the application by financial institutions of EDD to both foreign and domestic PEPs.[39] UNCAC has been signed by 140 States Parties, none of which have made a reservation to Article 52(1)—which means that all parties are obliged to enact measures for "enhanced scrutiny of accounts" for both domestic and foreign PEPs.

Adding further confusion to the issue, the Third EU Directive does not distinguish between domestic and foreign PEPs, but requires that firms identify and apply EDD to PEPs who reside outside the jurisdiction. As a result, the Directive does not require EDD for PEPs who reside inside the jurisdiction, even if they were entrusted with a prominent public function overseas.[40] FATF Recommendation 6, on the other hand, focuses on those "entrusted with prominent public functions in a foreign country" regardless of their country of residence. These approaches cannot be equated: the *location* of the public function associated with a PEP is separate and distinct from the *residency* of the function holder. The result is that a literal reading of the Third EU

---

38. UNCAC, Article 52(1); FATF 40 Recommendations, Recommendation 6, and Interpretative Note to Recommendation 6.

39. UNCAC, Article 52(1).

40. There may be other provisions that would make EDD obligatory, however Article 13(4) of the Third EU Directive states "In respect of transactions or business relationships with politically exposed persons *residing in another Member State or in a third country*, Member States shall require those institutions and persons covered by this Directive to…" [emphasis added] There is no reference in the Directive that adopts the FATF language "entrusted with prominent public functions in a foreign country." See also appendix C.

Directive does not capture the same PEPs as FATF Recommendation 6. For example, if the child of the minister of natural resources of country X is residing in country Y for the purpose of attending school or employment, the Third EU Directive would not require banks in country Y to perform EDD on the child's accounts. Applying the FATF definition, EDD would be required regardless of where the PEP resides. Considering that past corruption cases have revealed instances of corrupt officials laundering funds through family members and close associates residing abroad, this residency requirement is overly restrictive and results in the exclusion of PEPs that can be a significant risk to the banking sector.

Despite international obligations under UNCAC, most legislators have made a political decision not to classify domestic office holders as PEPs. Still, banks in some jurisdictions are expected to consider, on a risk-sensitive basis, whether domestic PEP customers pose a threat similar to that of their foreign counterparts. In the team's review of the 82 FATF and FATF-Style Regional Body (FSRB) mutual evaluation reports, 55 of the reports referred to laws, regulations, or guidance addressing foreign or domestic PEPs or both. Of these, 30 countries impose requirements only on foreign PEPs; 24 have requirements for both foreign and domestic PEPs.[41]

These opposite approaches need to be resolved, which raises the question as to the best approach. This policy paper advocates the removal of the distinction between foreign and domestic PEPs for three principal reasons:

First, the legal and reputational risks remain the same, whether the PEP is domestic or foreign. PEP controls are designed to draw attention to, and mitigate, the increased money laundering risk posed by this category of customer. While corruption is more prevalent in some countries than in others, domestic politicians are subject to the same pressures and perverse incentives as their foreign counterparts and should be treated accordingly. In some cases, the corrupt money may enter the financial system first through a bank in the victim country, and then through the correspondent relationships into the major banks in larger financial centers.

Second, although some have argued that covering both domestic and foreign PEPs would be too burdensome on banks, evidence gathered in the course of the visits suggests otherwise. Many of the banks most at risk of having corrupt PEPs as clients do not distinguish between foreign and domestic PEPs. In fact, most banks stressed that a distinction made little business sense and that it was easier to set up systems to include

---

41. One country imposes requirements for domestic PEPs only. Mutual evaluation reports from jurisdictions with laws, regulations, or guidance addressing foreign and domestic PEPs at the time of their most recent mutual evaluation report include Antigua and Barbuda, Argentina, The Bahamas, British Virgin Islands, Bulgaria, Cape Verde, Cayman Islands, Dominica, The Gambia, Grenada, Haiti, Indonesia, Malawi, Mauritius, Mexico, Montenegro, Pakistan, the Philippines, Qatar, Sierra Leone, South Africa, Thailand, the United Arab Emirates, and the Virgin Islands (u.s.). Brazil, although not included in the sample group, also imposes requirements for both foreign and domestic PEPs.

both domestic and foreign PEPs. Often it is easier and less resource intensive to identify domestic PEPs. In addition, they were also concerned about the reputational risk of banking a corrupt PEP more generally, a risk that exists equally among domestic and foreign PEPs.

Third, such efforts would increase the credibility of the governments' commitment to fighting corruption and money laundering, particularly the States Parties to UNCAC that have committed to treating domestic and foreign PEPs equally.

Principal Recommendation:

Laws and regulations should make no distinction between domestic and foreign PEPs. The standards adopted by FATF and regional and national standard setters should require similar enhanced due diligence for both foreign and domestic PEPs.

Family Members and Close Associates

Corrupt public office holders appear to be increasingly employing strategies to disguise their ownership of the corrupt assets, including using family members and close associates to launder their illicit funds. In many cases, members of a corrupt PEP's family, or their associates, undertake transactions and apply for goods and services on behalf of a PEP. It is, therefore, important that a PEP definition include close associates and family members in addition to the prominent public official. Of course, this raises the issue of how to define these two categories.

Unfortunately, family and close associates are defined differently among the standard setters. UNCAC includes as close associates both persons and companies that are related to the individual entrusted with the prominent public function, whereas the FATF 40+9 Recommendations are silent on the issue.[42] The Third EU Directive also provides additional clarification by adding joint beneficial ownership of legal entities or legal arrangements.[43] Regarding family members, UNCAC and FATF do not limit the degree of relationship, while the Third EU Directive focuses on immediate family members, which may not be sufficient in cultures and jurisdictions in which the extended family maintains very close ties.

---

42. United Nations General Assembly Fifty-eighth session, "Report of the Ad Hoc Committee for the Negotiation of a Convention against Corruption on the work of its first to seventh sessions: Interpretative notes to the official records (travaux préparatoires) of the negotiations of the United Nations Convention against Corruption (United Nations, New York, October 7, 2003) A/58/422/Add.1, para 50.
43. Directive 2006/70/EC, Article 2(3).

In addition, the requirements of the standard setters are not entirely clear on the treatment of family and close associates. While both the FATF 40+9 Recommendations and UNCAC refer to family members and [close] associates in the definition of a PEP and require the same amount of EDD as for the office holder, the literal terminology differs slightly because of the sentence structure.[44] One regulator indicated this may imply a distinction between prominent public functions on the one hand and family members and close associates on the other.

Recommendations:

- FATF should clarify the definition of PEPs to ensure that it includes family members and close associates along with holders of "prominent public functions."

- Jurisdictions should clarify the definition of PEPs to ensure that it includes family members and close associates along with holders of "prominent public functions."

Other Categories

UNCAC does not list categories of PEPs, however FATF does. A number of jurisdictions have attempted to provide direction to financial institutions and regulatory authorities on these definitions by setting out specific categories of positions. A number of banks include additional categories in their definition of PEPs, going beyond the requirements under law or regulation. One bank included senior decision makers from international and supranational organizations, public associations, media, religious organizations, and public enterprises and undertakings. The Wolfsberg Group has outlined a number of additional categories, including heads and other high-ranking officers holding senior positions in the armed forces, members of ruling royal families with governance responsibilities, senior executives of state-owned enterprises, and senior officials of major political parties. Heads of supranational bodies (for example, UN, IMF, World Bank), members of parliament, senior members of the diplomatic corps, and members of boards of central banks may also be considered to fall within the definition, but may be excluded on a risk-based approach.[45]

---

44. UNCAC expressly includes family and associates in the definition of PEPs, whereas the FATF definition states "PEPs are individuals who are or have been entrusted with prominent public functions in a foreign country. . . . Family members or close associates of PEPs involve reputational risks similar to those with PEPs themselves."
45. "Wolfsberg Frequently Asked Questions on Politically Exposed Persons," May 2008.

Sometimes the categories are too restrictive and limit the scope of the definition. For example, limiting "judicial officials" to supreme court judges is problematic in practice: If judges in the lower courts are corrupt, the case is unlikely to reach the level of the supreme court in the first place. In addition, there is ample opportunity for judges in lower courts to engage in corruption. Another example are those who hold political functions at a subnational level or state level in a country. Where the individual's political exposure is comparable to that of similar positions at the national level, the definition should encourage financial institutions to treat those customers as PEPs on a risk-sensitive basis.

Therefore, if a country has adopted a risk-based approach, it is important that banks themselves decide whether additional categories are relevant for their purposes. In doing so, banks should take into account the risks posed by the product, service, or transaction sought as well as other factors that have a bearing on money laundering and corruption risks. Where the risk is higher, the net will be cast wider. In addition, the regulatory authority should provide guidance in this area.

5. How Long Is a PEP Considered a PEP?

Neither the FATF 40+9 Recommendations nor UNCAC impose or recommend any time limits on the period of time that a customer remains a PEP after the prominent public official has left the position ("once a PEP, always a PEP"). While this may be appropriate in some circumstances (for example, with some heads of state), a prominent public official's career is often short-lived. Applying EDD measures to all former office holders—and their families and close associates—for an infinite time would be disproportionate.

This circumstance has led some jurisdictions to introduce time limits after which banks are no longer obliged to treat former PEPs automatically as high risk customers. One jurisdiction only requires EDD for current officials and their family members and close associates (that is, once the PEP leaves office, EDD can cease). However, the length of time after which a customer has left a prominent public function is not indicative of the relative money laundering risk associated with the business relationship.

Time limits are always artificial and pose problems: They can impart a false sense of security that a customer no longer poses an increased risk of money laundering.[46] Evidence suggests that corrupt PEPs do not cease to move proceeds of corruption after leaving office and some may continue to receive payments. Indeed, officials and their family members and close associates may wait until after leaving to move the funds. This problem is intensified the shorter the time period the PEP continues to be treated as a PEP.

Banks should, therefore, be encouraged to consider the ongoing PEP status of their customer on a case-by-case basis using a risk-based approach, and regulatory authorities should provide guidance on what this entails. In each of the banks visited, the period of time was likely to be several years, if not decades (for example, in the case of heads of state or other senior level PEPs). Where risk is low, banks can consider declassifying the relationship, but only after careful consideration of risks and involving senior management approval.

---

46. One bank indicated that it allowed declassification of a PEP after a set period of time without consideration of ongoing risk.

Principal Recommendation:

Where a person has ceased to be entrusted with a prominent public function, countries should not introduce time limits on the length of time the person, family member, or close associate needs to be treated as a PEP.

Good Practice

The creation of a designated PEP committee that meets regularly to discuss whether PEP customers who have left office continue to pose an increased risk of money laundering. Decisions of the committee are unanimous. (For a description of the committee, see the Good Practice "Establishment of a PEP Committee" in chapter 11 in part 3).

6. Identification of PEPs: Who to Check and When to Check

Who to Check?

The identification of PEPs requires effective CDD processes, including the identification of beneficial owners. Building on this requirement, financial institutions should have in place appropriate risk-management systems to determine whether a customer is a PEP. All banks interviewed applied PEP checks to all customers at the account opening stage and periodically to existing customers.

The general requirement is that a bank should have risk management systems to identify if the customer is a PEP, such as asking the necessary questions, performing a database check, referring to publicly available information, and so forth. Some banks, by the nature of the products and services they offer or the level of investment typically made, may have a lower risk of attracting PEP customers. Applying multiple checks in every case could be disproportionate to the risks and bring no results. In these circumstances, banks should use appropriate risk-management systems to focus greater efforts on the relationships that carry an increased money laundering risk. Regulatory authorities should provide appropriate guidance.

All jurisdictions visited said they require banks to check whether a beneficial owner is a PEP, although this requirement was not always explicitly set out in legislation. The team's review of the 82 FATF and FSRB mutual evaluation reports found that at the time of the assessment a number of jurisdictions were not required, by law or regulation, to check if the beneficial owner was a PEP—even though the Methodology for FATF Recommendation 6 considers this as "essential criteria."[47]

Recommendation:

Law or regulation should include a requirement to determine whether a beneficial owner is a PEP in accordance with the Methodology for FATF Recommendation 6.

---

47. Methodology for FATF Recommendation 6 states this "essential criteria" at 6.1: "Financial institutions should be required, in addition to performing the CDD measures required under R.5, to put in place appropriate risk management systems to determine whether a potential customer, a customer or the beneficial owner is a politically exposed person."

When to Check?

Banks should, of course, check whether a potential customer, existing customer, or beneficial owner, is a PEP. In the private banking institutions visited, this check was often made *before* the establishment of a business relationship; the account could not be opened until all relevant investigations, such as beneficial ownership and the PEP's identification, had been undertaken.

Existing clients sometimes become PEPs after they enter a business relationship, so it is essential that a bank's existing client base also be regularly checked for customers whose PEP status has changed. Some banks interviewed assessed their client list against PEP databases regularly to identify such individuals; others used public information about corrupt PEPs as a trigger for ad hoc database checks. Others checked existing customers for PEP status as part of the normal updating of know-your-customer (KYC) information. Once a PEP has been identified, senior management should decide whether to continue the business relationship, and if so, apply EDD measures in line with national legal and regulatory requirements.

Recommendation:

As part of their ongoing business processes, banks should ensure that they hold up-to-date information on their customers; and having appropriate risk management systems to check PEP status must form part of this process.

Good Practice

Some banks run their customer list against commercial or in-house PEP databases on a regular basis, often daily or weekly. This practice ensures that the bank captures those customers who attain PEP status after the customer take-on process. Once these customers are identified, they are then reviewed by senior management, placed on the PEP customer list, and EDD is applied.

One country required that their customers inform them should they, a family member, or a close associate become a prominent public official. This tool allows banks to capture new PEPs among their existing customers. However, this system should not be used exclusively, and banks should not rely solely on these declarations, but should have other means for identifying PEPs in their existing customer lists.

Many of the banks visited include a PEP check when a customer requests an additional product or specific service. This routine is particularly important if the risk of money laundering associated with the new product is considered to be higher than with existing products the customer holds. PEP checks should form part of this risk consideration.

7. Identification of PEPs: How to Check

Would a National or International List of PEPs Be Easier?

Many banks suggested that there should be a definitive list of all PEPs and called upon governments to compile lists of domestic PEPs. In their view, a list would provide a uniform and definitive basis against which to apply EDD measures, would be easier for governments to obtain, and would reduce costs of compliance for banks. One bank suggested that an international organization should then collect the country lists and disseminate a "world-wide list" because of the onerous burden of checking multiple databases. There are a few jurisdictions that make available a list of domestic PEPs.

While there may be good rationales for a national or international PEP list, this paper does not recommend them. The lists have limited utility because they only contain certain prominent public officials, not family members or close associates, and are quickly out-dated. Corrupt officials may use the list to target members of the opposition, as well as remove their own names and those of supporters. An overly broad list, such as a list of all public servants, would be unmanageable in some jurisdictions and for the banks that would have to review them. Classification of PEPs, as well as the extent of a person's close family and circle of associates, will differ depending on political, social, and cultural contexts within the varying jurisdictions. Most important there is a serious risk that banks may rely exclusively on the list, and subsequently fail to consider whether other customers pose an increased risk of laundering the proceeds of corruption. If such an approach is taken, a set list of PEPs would also make PEP checks easy to circumvent by launderers.

Where banks rely on such lists, they must be aware of their limitations (for example, inaccuracies, lack of updates) and should not rely upon the list as the only means of checking PEP status. Other CDD checks must also be conducted.

Identification of the Beneficial Owner: Will the True Owner Please Stand Up?

One of the difficulties emphasized in the context of PEP identification is determining the beneficial owner, the natural person(s) who ultimately own or control a customer or transactions, beneficiaries, controllers, or relevant third parties. Those with control include directors, trustees, guardians, attorneys, and protectors; relevant third parties include a settlor of a trust or founder of a foundation. It is particularly difficult when the contracting party is a legal or corporate entity, trust, or intermediary (see "General

Observations and Challenges" in part 1). Without knowledge of the beneficial owner, it is impossible for a bank to determine if it is servicing a PEP.

Both UNCAC and the FATF 40+9 Recommendations require that banks identify and verify beneficial owners as part of the CDD process.[48] In FATF Essential Criteria 6.1, banks are required to put in place appropriate risk-management systems to determine if the beneficial owner is a PEP. More recently, the G20 leaders called for the strengthening of FATF standards on beneficial ownership and transparency, issues which FATF will be considering as part of the preparation for the fourth round of mutual evaluations.[49] Legislation and regulations have been adopted in some jurisdictions, although diverse approaches have been taken. Some jurisdictions require that financial institutions identify the natural person behind the beneficial ownership structures. Others impose thresholds below which it is unnecessary for banks to determine beneficial ownership (for example, 25 percent). A number of jurisdictions have not yet adopted the necessary legislation. This must be addressed by requiring disclosure of the natural person who is the beneficial owner.

In practice however, the process of identifying the ultimate beneficiary is complex. The identity of the true beneficial owner and origin of the proceeds is often concealed through the misuse of corporate entities, including corporations, trusts, foundations, and limited liability partnerships. The use of intermediaries can further obscure the process and, in some jurisdictions, legislation permits this by allowing banks to rely on intermediaries with little or no information required from the underlying customer. In banks that apply the threshold approach to determining beneficial ownership (for example, where banks are required to check only the beneficial owners with a share greater than 25 percent), the corrupt PEP may have a great opportunity to conceal involvement. FATF has conducted a thematic study to identify, in respect of corporate vehicles, areas of vulnerability for money laundering, along with risk factors to assist countries in identification of misuse.[50] Additional work is needed to bring jurisdictions into compliance with FATF standards requiring procedures to identify the beneficial owners of legal entities formed within a jurisdiction.[51]

All of the interviewed banks have procedures for identification of the beneficial owner. Most banks indicated that they require identification of the ultimate owner, who must be a natural person; one bank admitted only to going "as far as possible." Similar to the process of assembling a customer profile, a combination of tools is used

48. UNCAC, Article 52; FATF 40+9 Recommendations, Recommendation 5.
49. G20, "Leaders' Statement, the Pittsburgh Summit," (September 24–25, 2009), para 42.
50. Financial Action Task Force, "The Misuse of Corporate Vehicle, Including Trust and Company Service Providers," (October 13, 2006). The StAR Initiative is currently undertaking a study on corruption and the misuse of corporate vehicles for release in mid-2010. For additional information see www.worldbank.org/star.
51. Jurisdictions must also provide information on the identity of the beneficial owners of legal entities to law enforcement in response to a request and on a timely basis.

to complete the identification and verification process, including company registers, shareholder registers, information from the contracting party, some commercial databases, and other publicly available sources.

In one jurisdiction, the customer is required to complete a written declaration of the identity and details of the beneficial owner(s)—a requirement pursuant to an agreement between the jurisdiction's bankers' association and signatory banks. The form is signed and dated by the contracting party and includes a statement that it is a criminal offense (document forgery) to provide false information on the form, with a penalty of up to five years or a fine. The form approach has been adopted by banks in other jurisdictions, even when not required by law or regulation. In the jurisdiction where the form is used, the prosecuting authority has prosecuted cases for forgery (that is, falsely establishing in a written document a fact with legal application or what is referred to as an 'intellectual lie').

The written declaration of beneficial ownership is a valuable tool for a number of reasons. It assists in focusing on the process of identification of the beneficial owner at the outset, not only for bank officials but also for the contracting party. It provides the background information that will assist the bank with verification, as well as in determining if the beneficial owner(s) is a PEP. It will assist regulatory authorities in evaluating beneficial ownership practices and enable better oversight of how banks are handling beneficial ownership issues. Finally, the requirement to sign under penalty of a criminal offense and, where appropriate, the additional consequence of nonconviction based or criminal forfeiture, serves to alert the contracting party to the seriousness and importance of the information and, therefore, acts as a deterrent. It may not be a deterrent for the corrupt PEP, but may be for intermediaries and others (including family and close associates) who are acting as the contracting party. Although it should be left up to each jurisdiction, regulatory authority, and financial institution to determine the most comprehensive means of identifying beneficial ownership, having a uniform document that records the customer's declaration of the beneficial owner would prove helpful. Uniform use of the form will assist in responding to domestic or foreign requests by authorities for account information. Use of the form also expands the information available to the names of beneficial owners (not just the names of the contracting party).

Some jurisdictions may not have defined a criminal offense that can be used for prosecuting a customer for lying to a financial institution or committing a fraud against it or the state regarding beneficial ownership (especially for state-owned or regulated institutions). In these cases, as well as where a criminal offense applies, the customer's signed declaration could still be used as: evidence of criminal intent in a money laundering or fraud prosecution, the basis for a civil suit by the financial institution, a reason for closing the account, and an important piece of evidence in a nonconviction based freezing or forfeiture proceeding initiated by the government. In the context of responding to domestic or foreign requests by authorities for account information, banks will be able to provide the name of the beneficial owner even if they are not the account holder.

Most banks and law enforcement agencies indicated that a written declaration would provide a valuable additional tool to assist with the identification and verification process, as well as enhance the audit trail and aid investigations. Given these factors, we consider the written declaration of beneficial ownership of all customers to be a critical first step—not the "silver bullet"—in the toolbox of items that will help in the identification and verification of beneficial ownership and form part of the overall customer due diligence policy.

Principal Recommendation:

At account opening and as needed thereafter, banks should require customers to complete a written declaration of the identity and details of the natural person(s) who are the ultimate beneficial owner(s) of the business relationship or transaction as a first step in meeting their beneficial ownership customer due diligence requirements.

A sample form is included in this paper (see box 2.2). Some of the key characteristics of such a declaration include the following:

- The contracting party must complete the declaration in writing and provide a signature to prevent subsequent claims of misunderstanding the question or errors in transcribing the information.
- The contracting party must declare *either* that he or she is the sole beneficial owner *or* provide the list of beneficial owners, thus requiring an intentional choice and act by the contracting party.
- The signature must be witnessed by a bank official. A witness is someone to identify the document and attest to the act of the contracting party completing it.
- The document must contain an assertion that a false statement is a criminal offense (when possible), as well as the applicable penalty and additional consequences (for example, nonconviction based or criminal forfeiture). In addressing whether to use existing laws or regulations or to add new ones, deliberate or willful ignorance should be additional grounds for prosecution. This puts the customer on notice of the consequences of providing material false information. The original signed document should be kept in accordance with the bank's requirements for document collection and must be accessible by relevant officials, including the anti-money laundering and combating the financing of terrorism (AML/CFT) compliance officer.
- A requirement to advise the bank of any change in the beneficial ownership, control, or links with the third party.
- A definition of beneficial owner that is as broad as possible should be included on the form, whether as defined by national law or by international standards or conventions.

BOX 2.2	**Sample Form for Declaration of Identity of the Beneficial Owner**

Form X: Declaration of Identity of the Beneficial Owner

[To be executed by the contracting customer in writing.]

Account/Deposit No.

Contracting customer: _____
[full name and address] _____

I, the contracting customer, hereby declare:
(mark with a "X" where appropriate)

❏ that I am the sole beneficial owner* of the assets in the account referenced above

OR

❏ that the beneficial owner(s) of the assets in the account referenced above is/are:
[Provide: Full name of the natural person(s), date and place of birth, nationality, address/domicile, country, passport number, national ID number, or similar national identification document and a copy of such documents]

_____
_____
_____
_____

The contracting customer undertakes to [automatically] [or within a reasonable period of time and in any event no less than two weeks] inform the Financial Services Business [insert applicable bank contact] in writing about any changes in the information provided above.

It is a criminal offense to [deliberately] [intentionally] provide material false information on this form [insert applicable criminal law and penalty in bold type].

Signature(s) of the contracting customer: Witnessed by bank official:

_____   _____

Date: _____   Name:_____

                                            Title:_____

                                            Date:_____

* Beneficial owner includes [the natural person(s) who ultimately owns or controls a customer and/or the person on whose behalf the transaction is being conducted. It also incorporates those persons who exercise ultimate effective control over a legal person or arrangement and relevant third parties. [Citations to national law, international standards, or conventions as appropriate.]

The written declaration is *one* tool—and far from the *only* tool—that banks will need to draw upon in identifying and verifying the beneficial owner. The written declaration is not sufficient on its own nor does it allow banks to be "off the hook" with respect to their obligations. Banks must take other steps to conduct CDD as well as to verify the content of the form, and regulators must ensure that banks are pursuing a number of avenues in determining this critical information.[52]

Identification Tools

Even after a customer is identified, determining if the individual holds a prominent public function can still be difficult, particularly if little public information is available from the individual's country of origin. The task is even more difficult with close associates and family members.

Banks usually have systems in place to determine the risk of money laundering associated with a particular business relationship and these tools should be adapted for the PEP context. These systems include generic indicators and information sources, such as risks associated with certain jurisdictions, products, the prominent public office holder's seniority, or area of business (such as arms dealing, trade in precious metals, or natural resource extraction of oil, timber, mining, and so forth). One of the key components of PEP identification is simple: Staff handling the business relationship need to have experience, use common sense, and demonstrate good judgment. Some of the processes that can be used to help identify PEPs include the following:

- *Customer due diligence.* The identification of a PEP customer usually results from a bank's normal CDD processes. Depending on the type of product or service sought, geographic area of business, or source of funds, CDD could also include questioning the customer on whether he or she is a PEP. Certain answers would normally trigger further research. One jurisdiction visited requires customers to sign a declaration of PEP status as part of account opening.
- *Transaction monitoring and ongoing monitoring.* As banks conduct ongoing monitoring of a business relationship, they may come across patterns that are difficult to explain, triggering further research into the customer's background. This investigation can lead to the identification of a PEP among existing clients (see also the "Enhanced Ongoing Monitoring" chapter in part 2).

Banks also have tools at their disposal to assist with the analysis of risk factors, such as country risk. A number of resources were referred to by banks as assisting in assessing country risk, including the World Bank List of Fragile States,[53] Transparency International's

---

52. Banks should keep a record of the different steps taken to determine beneficial ownership, as well as other CDD and EDD measures and, where appropriate, make this available to regulatory authorities and law enforcement. See FATF 40+9 Recommendations, Recommendation 10.
53. The World Bank List of Fragile States (2007) can be found at http://go.worldbank.org/HCP9BFLFL0.

Corruption and Perceptions Index (CPI),[54] and the FATF list of jurisdictions of concern. The FATF and FSRB mutual evaluation reports as well as the International Monetary Fund (IMF) and the World Bank AML/CFT assessments also provide detailed information on AML/CFT frameworks. If the bank, for example, is assessing business risk associated with natural resource extraction, information is available from the World Bank, the IMF Guide to Resource Revenues Transparency, or the Extractive Industries Transparency Initiative (EITI) on the status of resource governance and revenue transparency in some countries.[55]

A number of tools may be available to assist with name searches, including the following:

- *Business knowledge.* Some banks maintain a "black list" of business applicants who have been refused or terminated, as well as individuals whose names have been added based upon local knowledge or intelligence gathered in the course of business development (for example, while developing prospect lists).
- *Group compliance.* Some "black lists" are kept and shared at the group level.
- *Commercial PEP database providers* (see the "Identification of PEPs: Commercial and In-House Databases" chapter in part 2).
- *Asset and income declaration filing lists.* Some countries publish the income declarations of public officials or even a list of the names of filers (see box 2.3). The list may not include the names of some filers, for example, if national security or law enforcement concerns outweigh the benefit of publication of names.
- *Media and journals.*
- *In-country sources from the customer's country of origin.*
- *The Internet and search engines.* To complement searches conducted using large search engines, searches of smaller sources that could be linked to the customer may assist in locating relevant information (for example, media Web sites in the customer's country of origin).

Good Practice

If a country publishes a list of names of people who file asset and income declarations (the declaration itself may not necessarily be public), banks can use this information as another tool to assess whether a customer is a PEP.

As indicated earlier, the identification of the close associates who may be shielding a prominent public official is one of the most challenging issues. In this regard, it is critical for banks to know their customer. From this point of reference, banks need to understand the nature of the business transactions and whether these fit with the customer profile; and they need to understand source of wealth and source of funds

54. CPI is a list of countries ranked according to their perceived level of corruption.
55. See "International Monetary Fund: Guide on Resource Revenue Transparency (2007)." For information on EITI, see www.eitransparency.org/eiti. For information on the World Bank involvement in EITI, see http://go.worldbank.org/ZYUWPOA5E0.

| BOX 2.3 | The Use of Asset and Income Declarations for Identifying PEPs |

Asset and Income Declarations

Approximately 114 jurisdictions require their public officials to file declarations or disclosures of their assets and income with an ethics office, anticorruption body, or other government department.[a] The declarations usually contain information on the assets and income of public officials, including the sources of wealth and current business activities. The required information can also extend to a spouse or partner and children, and may include supporting documentation.[b] Some jurisdictions mandate that the forms be made available to the public; others do not.

UNCAC, Article 52(5) requires that States Parties consider establishing financial disclosure systems for appropriate public officials and appropriate sanctions for noncompliance.

At the same time, the declarations and their uses vary across the jurisdictions. Key issues include the accuracy of the information, particularly because many countries do not yet perform strong verification of these declarations. However, the declarations usually include information that can be useful in customer profiling. When they are used by banks, confidentiality of the information must be a priority.

Some Uses for Asset and Income Declarations

- Publication of the list of those who file asset and income declarations would provide banks with another search tool in efforts to identify PEPs.

- Elements relevant to the determination of source of wealth and source of funds.

- Regulatory authorities can provide guidance as to the availability and use of the declarations and, even if not required by legislation or regulation, can ask banks if they use the declarations. This inquiry will help in assessing how the bank is managing its PEP risk.

- FIUs can use the information in asset and income declarations to improve their analysis of suspicious transaction reports and national information can be shared through the Egmont Group of financial intelligence units.

a. Simeon Djankov, Rafael La Porta, Florencio Lopez-de-Silanes, and Andrei Schleifer, "Disclosure by Politicians," (National Bureau of Economic Research, Cambridge, MA, 2009) lists 109 countries that require members of parliament (MPs) to file asset and income declarations. Since publication of the paper, Dominica, Haiti, Iceland, the Seychelles, and Sierra Leone have added asset and income disclosure requirements for MPs. The paper is available at http://www.nber.org/papers/w14703.

b. For more information on asset and income declarations, see Ruxandra Burdescu, Gary Reid, Stuart Gilman, and Stephanie Trapnell, "Income and Asset Declarations: Tools and Trade-offs," (World Bank, Conference Edition released November 2009).

and whether this fits with the customer profile. Together this information may help to identify a close associate or distant family member. It would be helpful in this regard if regulatory authorities or financial intelligence units (FIUs) could develop "red flags" to guide banks in identifying close associates.

Some jurisdictions will permit reliance on intermediaries, such as accountants, lawyers, or trust and company services providers, with little or no information being disclosed. In these jurisdictions, it is important to limit this exemption in the case of underlying relationships that are high risk, particularly PEPs. One bank requires, for example, that the intermediary provide full CDD in relation to the underlying customer so that the bank can undertake its own acceptance and escalation process.

Recommendations:

- PEPs present a multi-dimensional or asymmetric risk to banks; therefore, banks should use a variety of risk factors and identification tools to ensure they have an effective approach to detect PEPs.

- Regulatory authorities or FIUs or both should develop "red flags" to guide banks in identifying close associates.

8. Identification of PEPs: Commercial and In-House Databases

The obligation to identify PEPs has prompted many banks to use resources such as commercial databases and other platforms that compile publicly available information. These databases and platforms compile and store information from a variety of open sources, including the Web sites of governments, international organizations, media, and sanctions lists. These resources provide information on public office holders and, in some cases, their legal entities, family members, and known associates. Software applications are often used in conjunction with the databases, particularly to screen large lists of clients. Some larger banks have developed in-house databases to complement the commercial database providers. Sources include publicly available information gathered through searches or downloaded from commercial databases as well as business information on individuals who the bank considers to be higher risk, such as those on bank "black lists."

Both advantages and challenges come with using these commercial databases and platforms. The advantages are their wide reach across a large number of jurisdictions, different language groups and characters, and the sheer size of the data set available. The information gathered is much more helpful, and often presented in a more user-friendly manner, than would be obtained through a simple search engine on the Internet. In addition, the databases and accompanying software application can offer a range of subscription options that can be tailored to the needs of the bank, from manual searches to automated batch-screening of a bank's entire customer account list or transactions. The accompanying software application can be sufficiently flexible to search for similar terms, rather than requiring an exact wording match, and can also restrict search criteria to certain categories of positions or jurisdictions.

However, a number of challenges remain. The databases do not contain all information because some areas of the world simply have less information available through news sources and the Internet. A challenge emphasized by a number of banks is the large volume of "hits" and false positives (for example, searching 5,000 names with a 10 percent match rate = 500 people; searching 10 million names with a 10 percent match rate = 1,000,000 people). One of the reasons for this large volume of information is the fact that the databases do not always have identifiers for the names, such as date of birth or sex, that would help reduce the number of false positives. The providers are aware of the issue and are adding identifiers; however, some are limited because of lack of information or they only collect open-source information (for example, from the Internet or in the media). For privacy reasons, they do not draw upon other information that may also be publicly accessible (such as birth registries). Finally, the entire package of services—the database, software, and staff to review the hits—can become quite a costly venture.

The conclusion from this review is that these databases provide a very helpful tool for banks. At the same time, the limitations are such that banks should not rely upon them as the *only* source for determining if a customer is a PEP. They are simply another tool for developing a complete picture of the customer. Other tools and processes will need to be considered, as outlined previously.

Some databases and software applications enable users to adjust the settings and parameters of their searches. This function allows a bank to search against a subset of the sources in the database (for example, individuals from one of the noncooperative countries and territories of FATF) rather than the entire database. Although changing the parameters can be helpful in lowering the number of false positives, banks must use caution because calibrating screening rules too narrowly increases the risk that PEPs are not identified.

Banks using automated systems for PEP screening should consider whether the screening rules are calibrated appropriately for the nature of the bank's business, attitude to risk, and customer list. If not, potential matches might not be identified. Regulatory authorities should review the settings of such databases and the specific reliance being placed on database results.

Recommendation:

Where applicable, the regulatory authority should include, as part of the onsite inspection, a review of the database used to identify PEPs. The review should include an examination of the commercial database parameters, sample transaction testing, and a review of the bank's overall database management practices.

Good Practice

Reviewing Database Search Parameters

One regulatory authority uses onsite examinations to assess the performance of PEP searches, including a review of the database search parameters, the algorithms being used for routine and ongoing monitoring purposes, and in-house search feeds.

9. Identifying and Verifying Source of Wealth and Source of Funds

Understanding a customer's source of wealth and source of funds is an important component of the EDD obligations that banks must apply to PEP customers.[56] The process provides key information that can assist a bank in determining whether a PEP is a legitimate customer. In addition, it contributes significantly to the customer profile that the bank will use as the "baseline" when conducting enhanced ongoing monitoring of the business relationship with a PEP.

Despite the importance of establishing source of wealth and source of funds, legislation and regulation do not always require that it be done. In addition, some of the FATF and FSRB mutual evaluation reports have drawn attention to the confusion on whether *both* concepts are included in the scope of the existing provisions. This lack of clarity leads to an inconsistent application of the standards among banks.

Recommendation:

To assist banks in meeting the source of wealth and source of funds requirement in the FATF 40+9 Recommendations in a consistent and meaningful manner, regulatory authorities should take steps to provide guidance to ensure both provisions are being addressed, and suggest ways in which a bank may go about applying them.

Similar to the process for identifying PEPs, it is critical that banks use a variety of tools to establish source of wealth and source of funds. The tools may include obtaining information directly from the customer, with corroboration through documentation (for example, contracts, agreements for lease or sale, wills, court orders, and asset and income declarations—described in box 2.3), Internet searches, and intelligence from

---

56. "Source of wealth" describes the activities that have generated the total net worth of the customer (that is, the activities that produced the customer's funds and property). "Source of funds" describes the origin and the means of transfer for funds that are accepted at account opening (for example, occupation, business activities, proceeds of sale, corporate dividends). See also "Wolfsberg AML Principles on Private Banking," 1.3. FATF 40+9 Recommendations, Recommendation 6(c) requires financial institutions "take reasonable measures to establish the source of wealth and the source of funds."

referrals or in-country sources (for example, another bank within the same banking group). Some jurisdictions require customers to complete a sworn statement in which they declare the source of their wealth at account opening. For particularly higher-risk PEP relationships, banks should take additional steps to corroborate the information, for example, by contracting with an external company to conduct investigations or a site visit to the place of business.

One helpful tool in determining the source of wealth and source of funds—as well as in developing a KYC profile—are the asset and income declarations that many PEP customers are required to file in their home jurisdictions (see box 2.3 for more information). These disclosures may provide information on the assets and income of public officials, including the source of wealth and current business activities.

If a bank is aware that a PEP customer is from a jurisdiction that requires its public officials to file asset and income declarations, the bank should request a copy. This request should be made regardless of whether the declaration is publicly available, because the onus is on the customer to provide the information. Legitimate reasons for a refusal or for not having filed may exist. The PEP may have privacy concerns about providing the declaration, especially in cases where the purpose of the account is limited, or may be prohibited by the government from sharing the declaration. Perhaps the PEP did not file the declaration in the first place out of concerns for safety and security, or is not permitted to share the form. In all cases, the bank should inquire about the reason for the refusal and determine, on a risk-sensitive basis, whether to continue the relationship. Where the declaration is provided, the bank must take steps to ensure confidentiality of the information.

A few sources can assist banks in determining the jurisdictions that require the filing of asset and income declarations by public officials. One is a paper entitled "Disclosure by Politicians," by Simeon Djankov, et al., which reviews the asset and income disclosures filed by members of parliament and provides a list of the countries that file in its appendix A.[57] Another tool is an Internet data portal of the Public Accountability Mechanisms Initiative of the World Bank that provides legislative information from approximately 75 countries on filings of heads of state, ministers and cabinet members, members of parliament, and civil servants.[58] It should be noted that analyses of international practices on asset declarations raise issues about the quality of many of those declarations. Still, it appears they may provide additional and complementary—though not definitive—information.

---

57. Simeon Djankov, Rafael La Porta, Florencio Lopez-de-Silanes, and Andrei Schleifer, "Disclosure by Politicians," (National Bureau of Economic Research, Cambridge, MA, 2009) lists 109 countries that require members of parliament (MPs) to file asset and income declarations. Since publication of the paper, Dominica, Haiti, Iceland, the Seychelles, and Sierra Leone have added asset and income disclosure requirements for MPs. The paper is available at http://www.nber.org/papers/w14703.
58. Internet portal address: www.agidata.org/pam/.

Principal Recommendation:

A public official should be asked to provide a copy of any asset and income declaration forms filed with their authorities, as well as subsequent updates. If a customer refuses, the bank should assess the reasons and determine, using a risk-based approach, whether to proceed with the business relationship.

Once the source of wealth and source of funds are established, banks will need to analyze the information for "red flags" for corrupt PEP activity. Because certain institutions, industries, and jurisdictions face higher money laundering or corruption risks, thus requiring additional caution, other relevant information will include the type of business and the geographical sphere of the activities that have generated a customer's wealth. If third-party funding is involved, banks should make further inquiries about the relationship between the person providing the funds and the customer.

In the event of doubt about the veracity of the information provided for either source of funds or source of wealth, the banks visited indicated they would not open the account or—in the case of an existing customer—would terminate the relationship. In all cases, if a bank suspects that the funds are proceeds of criminal activity, the bank is required to file a suspicious transaction report (STR) with the FIU (see FATF Recommendation 13).

Good Practice

Banks set guidelines for establishing source of wealth and source of funds to include requirements for verification and escalation in the event of lack of clarity or suspicion.

10. PEP Approval by Senior Management

The FATF standard requires banks to obtain senior management approval for establishing a business relationship with a PEP and continuing a business relationship with a customer who is subsequently found to be a PEP or becomes a PEP.[59] The exact meaning of the term, "senior management approval" is unclear. Some jurisdictions have either not provided any interpretation of the term or explained that such approval may be at the compliance, branch, or board of director level. In some jurisdictions, the AML/CFT compliance officer may also be a senior manager.

In addition to senior management, the group AML/CFT compliance officer (where existing) should be involved in the PEP approval process, at least in cases of higher risk, for two important reasons.[60] First, an AML/CFT officer is often in the best position to say that a person should not be accepted regardless of the size of the account. Second, involvement at the highest level is critical, especially in the context of information-sharing practices within the bank and group. In most banks visited, the individual members of the group can share information with the group office, but not with the other members of the group (that is, they can share with their "parents," but not with their "brothers and sisters"). The result is that the group AML/CFT compliance officer has broader information on the customer base, STRs filed across the group, terminated customers, and in some cases, refused customers. This top-level perspective prevents the acceptance of a customer who has already been refused or terminated at another location (customers who are branch or country-shopping).

Recommendation:

In higher risk cases, the group AML/CFT compliance officer (where existing), in addition to senior management, should be involved in the decision to accept or continue a relationship with a customer who has been identified as a PEP.

---

59. FATF 40+9 Recommendations, Recommendation 6(b).
60. In a number of banks, the group AML/CFT compliance officer is a senior manager.

With respect to the decision-making process, internal bank policies should outline who is involved and how (for example, unanimous agreement by all or a decision-tree approach in which the decision is approved at various levels). Most of the banks visited described a multilayered senior management approval process. In many cases, a new PEP relationship required separate approvals from the business and compliance unit heads. In some cases, a group compliance unit would have final approval over a new PEP account and in others, the final decision rested with a group business head. At one bank, there appeared to be about eight different units that were required to review a new PEP client, including final sign-off at the board level. Other banks had fewer layers, but built in various opportunities for escalation to separate committees or units (for example, reputation check or core business compliance unit at the broader group level) if a PEP was thought to immediately pose a higher risk or reside in a sensitive jurisdiction. Whatever the policy, it should be outlined in writing and decisions should be documented.

Good Practice

The decision at the senior management level to accept or continue a relationship with a customer identified as a PEP is documented, with clear delineation of responsibility and accountability. Approval or refusal by the various senior managers involved should be documented in writing.

11. Enhanced Ongoing Monitoring

Once a business relationship has been established with a PEP, banks must conduct enhanced ongoing monitoring[61] of the business relationship.[62] The FATF 40+9 Recommendations do not define enhanced ongoing monitoring beyond the need for senior management approval at initiation and the checks on the source of wealth and source of funds. Ongoing monitoring includes processes to monitor the PEP's transactions and evaluate whether the activity accords with the customer profile, as well as periodic updating of client information. Enhanced ongoing monitoring is also expected to entail an overall review of individual PEP customers by senior management. Beyond increasing the frequency of and attention to these processes because of the high risk category of a PEP, a number of PEP-specific practices are outlined below.

Transaction Monitoring

The process of monitoring transactions involves combining knowledge of the customer profile, source of wealth and source of funds, and all applicable risk factors with the capacity to evaluate whether the account activity is consistent with these factors. In addition to the assessment of transactions against a customer profile, some banks introduce specific typologies for money laundering, including typologies involving corrupt PEP activity into their account monitoring. Guidance on typologies from the regulatory authority or FIU, where appropriate, would be helpful.

Regulatory authorities can also provide guidance to banks on some of the common "red flags" in cases of corrupt PEPs.

Good Practice

In the wake of news of a scandal involving a high-profile PEP at another bank, one bank provided employees with specific "red flag" indicators that may be more common with PEPs:

---

61. The term "enhanced ongoing monitoring" is sometimes used to refer to the process of detecting if an existing customer has become a PEP. For the purposes of this paper, "enhanced ongoing monitoring" refers only to the process of monitoring customers who have already been identified as PEPs. For information on the former, see the "When to Check" section of chapter 6 in part 2.
62. FATF 40+9 Recommendations, Recommendation 6(d).

- activity inconsistent with customer profile, record of previous activities, or profile of businesses in same peer group;
- transactions over a certain value;
- sums deposited into the account are large relative to the wealth of the PEP and his or her family;
- funds transferred from an anonymous account (receiving bank should ask for identification details or reject the transaction);
- funds parked offshore;
- transfers from personal accounts to corporate accounts; transfers into or from an account of a third party or intermediary;
- complex ownership structures that hide the identity of the ultimate beneficial owner (for example, offshore nominee companies controlled by the nominee but indirectly under the PEP's control); and
- use of trust arrangements, especially when the settlor is also the beneficiary.

Awareness of PEP Customers: Maintaining Access to a List of PEP Customers

Although banks may not be required under regulation to maintain a list of their PEPs, the majority of the banks visited as part of the fieldwork either had a list or had the ability to generate one quickly. The list was often compiled by the AML/CFT compliance officer and held by the AML/CFT compliance officer or senior management or both. The list can assist with generating an overall view of PEP activity at a bank, and a number of banks have added other data fields to improve the usefulness of the list. Some regulatory authorities ask for the list as part of the onsite inspection—even if not required by regulation—because it contributes to the review of how the bank is managing its PEP risk, and can help the authorities in sampling during onsite examinations. Several banks indicated they keep an updated list of PEPs that includes the name of the PEP as well as a short KYC profile and the dollar value of assets in the accounts.

At the same time, the maintenance of a PEP list is not the sole indicator of effective risk management, nor is it the only tool for ongoing monitoring. Banks must ensure a comprehensive assessment of the risks of their PEP clients and engage other tools to assist in this process. Regulatory authorities must ensure that they look behind the list to see what the bank is doing: The generation of a list is insufficient in itself to show that a bank is successfully managing its PEP risk.

Recommendation:

An updated list of PEP accounts should be maintained by the AML/CFT compliance officer and be available to senior management.

Keeping the Customer Profile Updated

The customer profile should be kept up-to-date, whether through information gathered using automated database searches, manual updating of the customer profile, or transaction monitoring (manual or automated or both). Current information can reveal changes to the political function or business profile, significant or unusual transactions, changes in risk characteristics, notable reputation issues (for example, prosecution, litigation, negative media coverage), information on the beneficial owner, as well as background supporting documents. The banks visited refreshed customer profiles using a risk-based approach at least annually.

Periodic Review Process

The "big picture" for each PEP customer needs to be reviewed using a risk-based approach. All of the banks visited use this practice, with the timing ranging from frequent reviews to annual reviews. The process typically includes generation of a customer profile and portfolio report, as well as reports on the results of the transaction monitoring and changes to the customer profile. The reports are then analyzed by the account manager, compliance, head of business area, or through a sign-off process involving some or all the aforementioned (for example, members of a PEP committee, customer monitoring team). Finally, the information is considered by senior management or a committee including at least one senior manager. This individual or committee makes decisions on termination or continuation of the business relationship. Banks should also consider having the audit committee, board, or equivalent corporate governance body sign off on the PEP list annually.

Principal Recommendation:

PEP customers should be reviewed by senior management or a committee including at least one senior manager using a risk-based approach, at least yearly, and the results of the review should be documented.

Recommendation:

PEP customers should be reviewed annually by the audit committee, board or equivalent corporate governance body as part of its risk-management responsibilities.

To assist in the coordination of regular reviews and the decision-making process, a few banks have implemented a "PEP Committee." In one large bank, retail PEP accounts are transferred to a specific retail branch, which has responsibility for enhanced ongoing monitoring. These are simply a few examples of practices; a bank may pick a more suitable option based on its situation. Whatever the arrangement, these roles and responsibilities must be clearly outlined in the bank's policies.

Good Practice

Establishment of a PEP Committee.

One bank structured its PEP committee as follows:

- Authority
  - Make a record of all PEPs within the bank
  - Carry out a regular review of PEP customers
  - Provide opinions, on an annual basis, on whether to continue relationships with PEP customers
  - Make decisions on measures to be taken

- Members
  - chief executive officer (CEO)
  - head of compliance of the business area
  - records manager
  - customer manager
  - other occasional participants depending on the issue, such as the head of the business area

- Organization
  - Meets every two or three months, or at least quarterly, but also every time a permanent participant requests a meeting
  - Decisions are unanimous
  - Quorum is at least four of the participants, and must always include the CEO
  - Minutes of meetings are kept

PART 3
Role of Regulatory Authorities and the Financial Intelligence Unit

This part reviews the roles of the public authorities that are primarily involved in politically exposed persons (PEPs). These bodies include the regulatory authority, which is responsible for providing guidance to banks and assessing and enforcing compliance with PEP standards, and the financial intelligence unit (FIU), which has a role in the context of suspicious transaction reports (STRs) on PEPs.

There are a few overarching observations that apply to both regulatory authorities and financial intelligence units. Both require adequate resources and training (see also chapter 15 "Training and Resources" in part 4), as well as sufficient independence from political interference. Cooperation between the authorities is also critical (see also chapter 14 "National Cooperation" in part 4); and each of the jurisdictions visited stressed the importance of cooperation and communication in ensuring compliance by the regulated and reporting institutions.

12. Regulatory Authorities

Alongside a stringent legislative regime and an engaged and responsive private sector, a rigorous regulatory regime should be in place to ensure compliance by the private sector with legal and regulatory obligations.[63] Although specific controls can be put in place to prevent corrupt PEPs from using a financial services firm to launder the proceeds, these controls should form part of a jurisdiction's wider anti-money laundering (AML) controls. Without a comprehensive AML regime in place, specific PEP controls will not be effective.

Regulation of Bank PEPs Controls

In general, the regulatory bodies interviewed viewed PEPs controls as an integral part of a bank's AML regime. In situations in which regulatory authorities questioned banks about this issue, they usually did so in the context of their review of a bank's AML systems and controls. Only one regulatory authority had undertaken thematic projects specifically on PEPs; other authorities stated that PEPs form part of their ongoing regulatory procedures.

Thematic reviews focusing on PEPs as an issue can further the understanding of both the regulatory authorities and the regulated entities with regard to the current control environment surrounding PEPs in the jurisdiction. Thematic reviews can also help to ensure that regulators can identify weaknesses in banks or common challenges in implementation and issue guidance materials or best practices where appropriate. In jurisdictions where thematic reviews are conducted, they should at a minimum include work on AML controls and PEPs should form a part of the wider project.

Good Practice

One regulatory authority conducted a thematic review of systems and controls in relation to PEPs among a selection of banks in the jurisdiction. A report of the outcomes was published and made publicly available, outlining specific guidance and a regulatory framework in relation to PEPs, areas for improvement, and good practices.

---

63. This chapter focuses on some specific issues in supervision. For details of what the supervisor should be looking for in its assessment of bank compliance, please see part 2.

Recommendations:

- As part of its routine onsite assessments, the regulatory authority should include a focused PEP component and incorporate specific PEP questions, at least in those sectors or banks that are particularly exposed to PEPs. Such onsite assessments should be scheduled using a risk-based approach to effectively review changes in the current control environment.

- Regulatory authorities should conduct a PEP check on beneficial owners when assessing the "fit and proper" component at licensing.

Need for Additional Guidance from the Regulatory Authority

A number of the jurisdictions visited highlighted the need for open and constructive communication channels between key stakeholders in the public and private sectors and regulatory bodies with respect to expectations on how to deal with PEPs. Banks in the majority of the jurisdictions visited stated that they did not feel that the regulatory authority had issued enough guidance on their expectations. Banks also requested more information on the objectives of the rules and regulations in place.

The need for guidance should be partly addressed through an increased focus on PEPs, both within the ongoing regulatory process and as a specific strand of work. The information regulators continue to gather on the risks of PEPs and areas of vulnerability can be passed on to banks in the form of guidance. The results of any thematic work on either PEPs specifically or AML more generally should be published, giving a good indication of the expectations of the regulatory authority.

Recommendation:

Regulatory authorities should issue specific instructions that clearly outline the legal and regulatory obligations of banks in relation to PEPs. Regulatory authorities or FIUs or both should also disseminate typologies on "red flags" that could indicate corruption.

Good Practice

One regulatory authority informed banks in a guidance note that in cases of higher risks, the bank should expect an increased level of review by examiners to ensure that the institution has adequate controls and compliance oversight systems in place to monitor and manage such risks as well as personnel training for the management of such risks according to the requirements of applicable laws and regulations.

Sanctions

The fieldwork team noted a lack of regulatory sanctions imposed on banks for PEP deficiencies as well as general AML deficiencies in the jurisdictions visited. One authority suggested that the lack of sanctions was potentially a result of PEPs being part of a bank's wider AML system. Breaches of the PEP obligations were likely to be indicative of more fundamental problems with a bank's defenses and would result in sanctions for overall AML system failures rather than sanctions for PEP breaches. This argument makes sense, but it may also lead to insufficient feedback from the regulatory authorities on expectations regarding PEP requirements.

Conversely, the lack of PEP sanctions may be attributable, in part, to a lack of regulatory focus on PEPs. The fact that few of the banks visited cited the risk of regulatory action as a driver of compliance with PEP standards also points to the lack of regulatory focus. In this context, graduated regulatory sanctions (including punitive sanctions) are an effective tool for generating improvements in the industry—they send a signal to the private sector about key issues that the regulator views as important.

13. Suspicious Transaction Reporting and Financial Intelligence Units

Suspicious transaction reports or suspicious activity reports play a critical role in the fight against corruption and money laundering. Often an STR acts as a first warning signal of suspicious or unusual activity by a customer, and after analysis, can mobilize interagency cooperation between various regulatory, law enforcement, investigative, and prosecutorial bodies.[64] The team's discussions with government agencies, regulators, FIUs, investigators, prosecutors, and banks revealed that the STR is an important part of the PEP discussion.

Although FIUs recognize business relationships with PEPs as a potential corruption and money laundering risk, only limited efforts have been made to single out PEPs as a distinct FIU issue. Very few FIUs are able to collect reliable statistics on PEP-related STRs (PEP STRs), resulting in a lack of information on the scale of the problem and the effectiveness of the system in detecting it. In addition, written guidance is sometimes lacking on filing PEP STRs or typologies.[65]

The data available reveal a low number of PEP STRs relative to the total number of STRs. Uneven reporting rates within jurisdictions also occur, with a handful of banks submitting the majority of PEP STRs. Some banks suggested that the low number of STRs made sense because banks have a low number of PEP customers in the first place: If the number of PEPs is low as a percentage of total clients, so will be the number of STRs. At the same time, little data support this (for instance, little data exist on actual numbers of PEPs and PEP STRs). In addition, other indicators could influence filing rates, such as risks, guidance, and enforcement.

The increased international attention to the risks imposed by PEPs has prompted many FIUs to strengthen their resolve in this regard. The balance seems to be shifting toward greater focus on PEPs, but there is still significant room for improvement.

---

64. Cooperation may occur through an interagency STR review committee. Various investigators and prosecutors meet to determine if an STR should be investigated or prosecuted and who should take the lead.
65. Although FIUs generally carry out the three core functions of receiving, analyzing, and disseminating STRs, they vary in their administrative set-up and the types of guidance they can provide.

FIU Guidance to Reporting Institutions

To enable the FIU to collect accurate statistics on PEP STRs, guidance should be in place on how banks are to report PEP STRs, as well as the definition of PEPs; why the definition is important; and so forth. During the field visits, there were two main methods for including this information in the STR: using "key words" in the narrative and checking a "PEP box." Both approaches were used in all styles of STRs, whether the FIU required banks to complete a form or provide a narrative on the activity.[66] In the key-words approach, the FIU asks the banks to include certain terms in the narrative portions of STRs if the transaction is related to a PEP ("foreign corruption" is used by one FIU). With the PEP-box approach, the bank is required to check a box when the transaction is related to a PEP.

Based on discussions with banks and FIUs, the key-words approach is the most useful overall. The PEP-box approach can be too restrictive because less narrative information is provided—information that can provide important background for analysis of the STR. In all PEP STRs, even those with a PEP-box, FIUs should focus on helping banks to improve the narrative, including using certain key-words to identify PEP activity.

FIUs can use a number of additional mechanisms to provide guidance: formal guidance papers and circulars, including a thematic circular on PEPs; typologies on corruption and AML schemes that involve the suspicious activities of a PEP; feedback on STRs; and a direct line that reporting institutions can use to consult with FIU personnel and obtain guidance on specific cases.

Recommendation:

FIUs should provide guidance to banks on completing PEP STRs along with a glossary of key-words to be used in STR narratives.

Gathering Information

Accurate statistics are essential for understanding the scope of PEP risks and the effectiveness and efficiency of the system for detecting them.[67] In addition to collecting the number of PEP STRs, there could also be a breakdown on whether the PEP was a

---

66. Some FIUs have developed an STR form that includes specific fields to be completed, such as the name of the beneficial owner, products being used, date and location of activity, reason for suspicion, and so forth. Other FIUs rely on the financial institution to provide a detailed narrative description of the suspicious activity and any other information they deem relevant.
67. FATF 40+9 Recommendations, Recommendation 32 requires countries to maintain statistics on among other things, STRs, investigations, prosecutions, and convictions as a means of measuring effectiveness.

prominent public official, a family member, or a close associate. For additional statistics, the FIU will need to consider whether it needs to provide guidance to the industry on other key-words to use in the narrative.

The Egmont Group of Financial Intelligence Units is a forum for FIUs around the world to improve cooperation and the sharing of financial intelligence information in the fight against money laundering and financing of terrorism.[68] The Egmont Group should emphasize the importance of accurate and comprehensive statistics on PEP STRs as a means to assess risks and ultimately improve effectiveness.

One possible tool to assist in the analysis of PEP STRs is the PEP customer's asset and income declaration (see box 2.3 for an explanation on asset and income declarations). FIUs should be able to use this information for domestic PEPs. To analyze STRs related to foreign PEPs, the FIU may be able to access the declaration if it is publicly available; if access is limited to national law enforcement and national FIUs, it may be possible for the foreign FIU to obtain a copy using the Egmont Group's channels.[69] As indicated earlier, remaining issues with the quality and veracity of these asset and income declaration forms require caution; however, the information is still worth including in the analysis.

Recommendations:

- FIUs should maintain accurate, comprehensive, and public statistics on PEP STRs.

- FIUs should use asset and income declarations as a tool in their analysis of STRs.

- The Egmont Group should emphasize the importance of accurate and comprehensive statistics on PEP STRs as a means to assess risks and carry out strategic analysis within a given financial system.

---

68. For more information on the Egmont Group see www.egmontgroup.org.
69. This exchange may not be possible with all FIUs.

PART 4

National Cooperation, Training, and Resources

14. National Cooperation: Agencies and the Industry

The success of any politically exposed persons (PEPs) policy requires the commitment and ongoing collaboration of all actors involved—legislators, regulators, law enforcement agencies, and the private sector (including all reporting entities). Some jurisdictions have several regulatory authorities involved in establishing and monitoring anti-money laundering (AML) controls (including as it pertains to PEPs) as well as different law enforcement agencies that are responsible for the investigation and prosecution of money laundering or corruption cases. Encouraging interagency cooperation and harmonized standards in the issuance of PEP guidance by various authorities to the private sector is crucial.

At the outset, the government needs to make political and resource commitments to tackle corruption. Political will is critical to integrating national efforts into a single and consistent strategy and motivates regular and close communication between all concerned.

Trust, confidence, and reciprocity among law enforcement entities (including financial intelligence units [FIUs]), regulatory authorities, and the private sector are key features for effective implementation of PEP policies. This process is facilitated by a clear division of responsibilities between agencies operating in the AML regime, under a common and shared objective.

Good Practice

Partnering with other authorities and the private sector on PEP issues. One government has established a number of groups to address PEP issues.

Partnering with authorities on government strategy. A standing PEP group brings together all stakeholders at the governmental, law enforcement, and regulatory levels to coordinate the government's PEP initiatives and to provide a forum for the exchange of intelligence and good practices. Among other activities, this group developed a document setting out the government's rationale for engaging in the issue and started a communication strategy aimed at demonstrating the government's commitment to tackling money laundering by corrupt PEPs.

Partnering with other authorities on cases. An interagency group works exclusively on PEPs and corruption and includes the regulator, law enforcement, and various related agencies. It is a coordinating and information sharing body that looks at current cases to determine how best to manage them.

Partnering with the private sector. A group of high-level representatives of all major stakeholders, including public authorities and the private sector, focuses on the implementation of a PEP delivery plan with four objectives: communications, optimizing self-support by banks, regulatory environment, and enforcement.

Most jurisdictions visited in the framework of this project have established a close partnership on general issues, and a few in the context of PEPs. Some have strategically examined the PEP issue as part of their national agenda on money laundering, while others have created specific and ad hoc national PEP partnerships to work on comprehensive and coherent implementation of PEP standards.

Partnering with the private sector is critical in assessing the effectiveness of PEP systems and controls. The private sector should be involved in a number of relevant areas, for example, discussions of implementation issues, trends, typologies, and improving suspicious transaction reporting.

Recommendation:

Countries should build partnerships between public entities and representatives from the private sector to focus on the implementation of PEP policies and challenges and possibly discuss suspicious indicators, typologies, and trends.

15. Training and Resources

The PEP issue is one of many money laundering related risks of which banks, regulators, FIUs, and other public authorities must be aware. However, with the current lack of effective implementation of PEP standards by both national authorities and banks, specific attention must be given to training and adequate resourcing of all the relevant stakeholders. For banks in particular, efforts should focus on those institutions that are more likely, by the nature of their products and services or geographical representation, to have PEPs as customers.

The effectiveness of any AML strategy and PEP regime depends on the extent to which staff—whether at the banks, the regulatory authority, or the FIU—fully recognize the risks and understand the background against which PEP standards have been developed and have the tools to effectively detect and monitor PEPs. Training and adequate resources are critical in this regard, and the FATF 40+9 Recommendations require that both financial institutions and national authorities receive training and allocate sufficient resources.[70]

In all jurisdictions, political will at the highest levels is critical to fighting corruption and denying corrupt PEPs access to the financial system. Although the banks and authorities visited did not report issues with the allocation of adequate resources, there are many jurisdictions, authorities, or banks where additional resources are needed.

Training efforts need to ensure a proper focus. The field visits revealed that the factors driving compliance with PEP standards were reputational risk and, to a lesser degree, regulatory risk of enforcement action. Both factors are risks of "getting caught"— whether in a public scandal or for lack of enforcement—and are less focused on the risk of corruption and financial crime. To address these concerns, more awareness-raising campaigns should be organized around the potential dangers posed by these high-risk customers, stressing the corrosive aspects of corruption on societies and violations of human rights. An important approach taken by some banks has been to focus on creating a culture of compliance in which AML is treated seriously, even in the face of lost profits. Training is crucial in building and cementing this culture.

---

70. FATF Recommendation 15 requires that "financial institutions develop programs against money laundering and terrorist financing . . . [that] include . . . an ongoing employee training programme." FATF Recommendation 30 applies to supervisors and requires that they have "adequate financial, human and technical resources." Essential criteria 30.3 requires that staff have adequate and relevant training.

Good Practice

One bank uses a short video presentation to address the question "Why monitor PEPs?" The video gives an overview of the destructive effects of corruption around the world.

Bank staff have a crucial role to play in identifying customers who are PEPs, and regulatory authorities must enforce these obligations. It is, therefore, essential that regulatory authorities and banks develop policies on their relevant roles and thoroughly communicate these policies to employees (for example, onsite supervisors, desk officers, compliance, middle and senior managers). Training should be integrated into the AML programs and should be part of a bank's or regulator's induction and regular ongoing training regimes. Various types of training should be contemplated, including face-to-face, online modules, practical exercises, and case studies relating to specific PEP issues. In-depth training concerning PEP policies, national laws and regulations, use of commercial databases, as well as financial crime and PEP-related suspicious transaction indicators should be provided to individuals who may be addressing PEP detection and monitoring regularly, such as anti-money laundering and combating the financing of terrorism compliance officers.

FIUs should support the industry, provide guidance, and hold targeted training for reporting entities in addition to encouraging open and informal collaboration with banks on a case-by-case basis. Most banks interviewed have requested further support on how to identify corruption-related trends through typology reviews, which should also be incorporated into training modules (see also "Suspicious Transaction Reporting and Financial Intelligence Units" in part 3).

Good Practice

FIUs, in conjunction with prosecutors and law enforcement, provide tailored PEP training as part of a country's general AML program. The training includes general background that places corrupt PEPs in a wider context, explaining the rationale and need for internal policies, and the harm caused to society by corrupt behaviors and other criminal conduct. This includes a review of PEP "red flags," including for identifying close associates.

Appendix A: Summary of Recommendations— Quick Reference Sheet

Principal Recommendations

1. Laws and regulations should make no distinction between domestic and foreign PEPs. The standards adopted by FATF and regional and national standard setters should require similar enhanced due diligence for both foreign and domestic PEPs.

2. At account opening and as needed thereafter, banks should require customers to complete a written declaration of the identity and details of the natural person(s) who are the ultimate beneficial owner(s) of the business relationship or transaction as a first step in meeting their beneficial ownership customer due diligence requirements.

3. A public official should be asked to provide a copy of any asset and income declaration forms filed with their authorities, as well as subsequent updates. If a customer refuses, the bank should assess the reasons and determine, using a risk-based approach, whether to proceed with the business relationship.

4. PEP customers should be reviewed by senior management or a committee including at least one senior manager using a risk-based approach, at least yearly, and the results of the review should be documented.

5. Where a person has ceased to be entrusted with a prominent public function, countries should not introduce time limits on the length of time the person, family member, or close associate needs to be treated as a PEP.

Risk-Based Approach

6. Countries should carefully consider whether a risk-based approach will produce the best results. In doing so, they should consider the extent to which qualitative information that could inform risk assessments is readily available, the ability of the regulator to supervise and guide the sector, and the extent to which banks are equipped with sufficient resources and expertise to identify and mitigate any money laundering and PEP risks they face.

7. Where a risk-based approach is applied, regulatory authorities need to make efforts to ensure that the entire sector understands the approach and is applying it correctly, including in the context of PEP systems and controls.

Who Is a PEP?

8. FATF and UNCAC should align the definition of PEPs. This definition should be adopted by national standard setters and other key stakeholders.
9. FATF should clarify the definition of PEPs to ensure that it includes family members and close associates along with holders of "prominent public functions."
10. Jurisdictions should clarify the definition of PEPs to ensure that it includes family members and close associates along with holders of "prominent public functions."

Who to Check and When to Check?

11. Law or regulation should include a requirement to determine whether a beneficial owner is a PEP in accordance with the Methodology for FATF Recommendation 6.
12. As part of their ongoing business processes, banks should ensure that they hold up-to-date information on their customers; and having appropriate risk management systems to check for PEP status must form part of this process.

How to Check?

13. PEPs present a multi-dimensional or asymmetric risk to banks; therefore, banks should use a variety of risk factors and identification tools to ensure they have an effective approach to detect PEPs.
14. Regulatory authorities or FIUs or both should develop "red flags" to guide banks in identifying close associates.

Commercial and In-house Databases

15. Where applicable, the regulatory authority should include, as part of the onsite inspection, a review of the database used to identify PEPs. The review should include an examination of the commercial database parameters, sample transaction testing, and a review of the bank's overall database management practices.

Identifying and Verifying Source of Wealth and Source of Funds

16. To assist banks in meeting the source of wealth and source of funds requirement in the FATF 40+9 Recommendations in a consistent and meaningful manner, regulatory authorities should take steps to provide guidance to ensure both provisions are being addressed and suggest ways in which a bank may go about applying them.

PEP Approval by Senior Management

17. In higher risk cases, the group AML/CFT compliance officer (where existing), in addition to senior management, should be involved in the decision to accept or continue a relationship with a customer who has been identified as a PEP.

Enhanced Ongoing Monitoring

18. An updated list of PEP accounts should be maintained by the AML/CFT compliance officer and be available to senior management.
19. PEP customers should be reviewed annually by the audit committee, board, or equivalent corporate governance body as part of their risk-management responsibilities.

Regulatory Authorities

20. As part of its routine onsite assessments, the regulatory authority should include a focused PEP component and incorporate specific PEP questions, at least in those sectors or banks that are particularly exposed to PEPs. Such onsite assessments should be scheduled using a risk-based approach to effectively review changes in the current control environment.
21. Regulatory authorities should conduct a PEP check on beneficial owners when assessing the "fit and proper" component at licensing.
22. Regulatory authorities should issue specific instructions that clearly outline the legal and regulatory obligations of banks in relation to PEPs, as well as typologies on "red flags" that could indicate corruption.

Suspicious Transaction Reports and Financial Intelligence Units

23. FIUs should provide guidance to banks on completing PEP STRs along with a glossary of key-words to be used in STR narratives.
24. FIUs should maintain accurate, comprehensive, and public statistics on PEP STRs.
25. FIUs should use asset and income declarations as a tool in their analysis of STRs.
26. The Egmont Group should emphasize the importance of accurate and comprehensive statistics on PEP STRs as a means to assess risks and carry out strategic analysis within a given financial system.

National Cooperation: Agencies and the Industry

27. Countries should build partnerships between public entities and representatives from the private sector to focus on the implementation of PEP policies and challenges and possibly discuss suspicious indicators, typologies, and trends.

Appendix B: Summary of Good Practices— Quick Reference Sheet

How Long Is a PEP Considered a PEP?

1. The creation of a designated PEP committee that meets regularly to discuss whether PEP customers who have left office continue to pose an increased risk of money laundering. Decisions of the committee are unanimous.

Who to Check and When to Check?

2. Some banks run their customer list against a commercial or in-house PEP databases on a regular basis, often daily or weekly. This practice ensures that the bank captures those customers who attain PEP status after the customer take-on process. Once these customers are identified, they are then reviewed by senior management, placed on the PEP customer list, and EDD is applied.

How to Check?

3. If a country publishes a list of names of people who file asset and income declarations (the declaration itself may not necessarily be public), banks can use this information as another tool to assess whether a customer is a PEP.

Commercial and In-house Databases

4. One regulatory authority uses onsite examinations to assess the performance of PEP searches, including a review of the database search parameters, the algorithms being used for routine and ongoing monitoring purposes, and in-house search feeds.

Identifying and Verifying Source of Wealth and Source of Funds

5. Banks set guidelines for establishing source of wealth and source of funds to include requirements for verification and escalation in the event of lack of clarity or suspicion.

PEP Approval by Senior Management

6. The decision at the senior management level to accept or continue a relationship with a PEP is documented, with clear delineation of responsibilities and accountabilities. Approval or refusal by the various senior managers involved is documented in writing.

Enhanced Ongoing Monitoring

7. In the wake of news of a scandal involving a high-profile PEP at another bank, one bank provided employees with specific "red flag" indicators for PEPs.
8. Establishment of a PEP committee.

Regulatory Authorities

9. One regulatory authority conducted a thematic review of systems and controls in relation to PEPs among a selection of banks in the jurisdiction. A report of the outcomes was published and made publicly available, outlining specific guidance and a regulatory framework in relation to PEPs, areas for improvement, and good practices.
10. One regulatory authority informed banks in a guidance note that in cases of higher risks, the bank should expect an increased level of review by examiners to ensure that the institution has adequate controls and compliance oversight systems in place to monitor and manage such risks, as well as personnel training for the management of such risks according to the requirements of applicable laws and regulations.

National Cooperation: Agencies and the Industry

11. Partnering with other authorities and the private sector on PEP issues.

Training and Resources

12. One bank uses a short video presentation to address the question "Why monitor PEPs?" The video gives an overview of the destructive effects of corruption around the world.
13. FIUs, in conjunction with prosecutors and law enforcement, provide tailored PEP training as part of a country's general AML program. The training includes general background that places corrupt PEPs in a wider context, explaining the rationale and need for internal policies, and the harm caused to society by corrupt behaviors and other criminal conduct. This includes a review of PEP "red flags," including for identifying close associates.

Appendix C: Comparison of the PEP Definitions and Enhanced Due Diligence Requirements

The two main standards on PEPs, UNCAC and the FATF 40+9 Recommendations, and the Third EU Directive, have different definitions of PEPs and varying degrees of detail on the types of positions that would be included in a "prominent public function." Table A1.1 compares the PEP definitions set out in UNCAC, FATF, and the Third EU Directive, as well as some of the more specific examples of "prominent public functions." Other groups, including the Basel Committee on Banking Supervision and the Wolfsberg Group have also introduced definitions (see the section following table A1.1).

The three standards have also specified different enhanced due diligence requirements that must be taken with respect to PEPs, as illustrated in table A1.2.

Table A1.1 Comparison of the PEPs Definitions among the Standard Setters

	UNCAC[a]	FATF[b]	Third EU Directive[c]
Basic definition	Individuals who are, or have been, entrusted with prominent public functions and their family members and associates[d]	Individuals who are or have been entrusted with prominent public functions in a foreign country.... ... Business relationships with family members or close associates of PEPs involve reputational risks similar to those with PEPs themselves	Natural persons who are, or have been, entrusted with prominent public functions and immediate family members, or persons known to be close associates of such persons[e]
EDD required for foreign or domestic PEPs	Foreign and domestic (not explicit)	Foreign only[f]	PEPs residing in another country[g]
Time period after which there is no obligation to consider a PEP as a PEP	Not specified	Not specified	One year, on a risk-based approach[h]

(*Table continues on the following page.*)

Table A1.1 (continued)

	UNCAC[a]	FATF[b]	Third EU Directive[c]
Family members	Not specified	Not specified	Immediate family members[i] shall include: (a) the spouse; (b) any partner considered by national law as equivalent to the spouse; (c) the children and their spouses or partners; (d) the parents
Close associates	Persons or companies clearly related to individuals entrusted with prominent public functions[j]	Not specified	Close associates[k] shall include: (a) any natural person who is known to have joint beneficial ownership of legal entities or legal arrangements, or any other close business relations, with [a PEP]; (b) any natural person who has sole beneficial ownership of a legal entity or legal arrangement, which is known to have been set up for the benefit de facto of [a PEP]
Heads of state	Not specified	Heads of state	Heads of state[l]
Heads of government	Not specified	Heads of government	Heads of government[m]
Ministers and members of parliament	Not specified	No, but does include senior politicians and senior government officials	Ministers and deputy or assistant ministers; members of parliament[n]
Political parties	Not specified	Important political party officials	Not specified
Judiciary	Not specified	Judicial officials	Members of supreme courts, of constitutional courts, or of other high-level judicial bodies whose decisions are not subject to further appeal, except in exceptional circumstances[o]

Table A1.1 (continued)

	UNCAC[a]	FATF[b]	Third EU Directive[c]
Military	Not specified	Military officials	High-ranking officers in the armed forces[p]
State-owned enterprises	Not specified	Senior executives of state-owned corporations	Members of the administrative, management, or supervisory bodies of state-owned enterprises[q]
Diplomatic representatives	Not specified	Not specified	Ambassadors, chargés d'affaires[r]
Central bank boards	Not specified	Not specified	Members of courts of auditors or of the boards of central banks[s]
Exclusions	No explicit exclusions	Middle ranking or more junior individuals	Middle ranking or more junior officials[t]

Source: Authors' compilation.

Note:

a. The UNCAC definition is in Article 52(1) and (2), UNCAC. Although not explicitly referenced in Article 52, the definition "public official" in Article 2 of UNCAC can be of assistance: "… (i) any person holding a legislative, executive, administrative or judicial office of a State Party, whether appointed or elected, whether permanent or temporary, whether paid or unpaid, irrespective of that person's seniority; (ii) any other person who performs a public function, including for a public agency or public enterprise, or provides a public service, as defined in the domestic law of the State Party and as applied in the pertinent area of law of that State Party; (iii) any other person defined as a 'public official' in the domestic law of a State Party. However, for the purpose of some specific measures contained in chapter II of this Convention, 'public official' may mean any person who performs a public function or provides a public service as defined in the domestic law of the State Party and as applied in the pertinent area of law of that State Party."

b. The FATF definition is in the "Glossary of Definitions Used in the Methodology."

c. The definition of PEPs and specific examples are outlined in two Directives: Directive 2005/60/EC of the European Parliament and of the Council of October 26, 2005, on the prevention of the use of the financial system for the purpose of money laundering and terrorist financing (Dir 2005/60/EC); Commission Directive 2006/70/EC of August 1, 2006, laying down implementing measures for Directive 2005/60/EC with regard to the definition of "politically exposed person" and the technical criteria for simplified customer due diligence procedures and for exemption on grounds of a financial activity conducted on an occasional or very limited basis (Directive 2006/70/EC). For a copy of the directives, see appendix F.

d. UNCAC, Article 52(1).

e. Directive 2005/60/EC, Article 3(8).

f. See FATF glossary.

g. Directive 2005/60/EC, Article 13(4).

h. Directive 2006/70/EC, Article 2(4).

i. Directive 2006/70/EC, Article 2(2).

j. United Nations General Assembly, "Interpretative notes for the official records (travaux préparatoires) of the negotiation of the United Nations Convention against Corruption," (A/58/422/Add.1), para. 50.

k. Directive 2006/70/EC, Article 2(3).

l. Directive 2006/70/EC, Article 2(1)(a).

m. Directive 2006/70/EC, Article 2(1)(a).

n. Directive 2006/70/EC, Article 2(1)(a) and (b).

o. Directive 2006/70/EC, Article 2(1)(c).

p. Directive 2006/70/EC, Article 2(1)(e).

q. Directive 2006/70/EC, Article 2(1)(f).

r. Directive 2006/70/EC, Article 2(1)(e).

s. Directive 2006/70/EC, Article 2(1)(d).

t. Directive 2006/70/EC, Article 2(1).

The Basel Committee on Banking Supervision and the Wolfsberg Group have also introduced definitions as follows:

Basel Committee: "Individuals who are or have been entrusted with prominent public functions, including heads of state or of government, senior politicians, senior government, judicial or military officials, senior executives of publicly owned corporations and important political party officials."[71]

Wolfsberg Group: "Referring to individuals holding or having held positions of public trust, such as government officials, senior executives of government corporations, politicians, important political party officials, etc., as well as their families and close associates."[72]

The Wolfsberg Group has outlined a number of categories, including heads of state, heads of government and ministers, senior judicial officials, heads and other high-ranking officers holding senior positions in the armed forces, members of ruling royal families with governance responsibilities, senior executives of state-owned enterprises, and senior officials of major political parties. Heads of supranational bodies (for example, UN, IMF, World Bank), members of parliament, senior members of the diplomatic corps, or members of boards of central banks may also be considered to fall within the definition, but may be excluded on a risk-based approach.[73]

Table A1.2 Comparison of Enhanced Due Diligence Requirements

	UNCAC	FATF	Third EU Directive
EDD required for foreign or domestic PEPs	Foreign and domestic (not explicit)	Foreign only[a]	Foreign only[b]
Time period after which there is no obligation to consider a PEP as a PEP	Not specified	Not specified	One year, on a risk-based approach[c]
Identify PEP	Not specified	Have appropriate risk management systems to determine whether the customer is a politically exposed person	Have appropriate risk-based procedures to determine whether the customer is a politically exposed person[d]

---

71. Basel Committee on Banking Supervision, "Customer Due Diligence for Banks," (Bank for International Settlements, October 2001), para. 41.
72. The Wolfsberg Group, "Wolfsberg AML Principles on Private Banking," para 2.2.
73. "Wolfsberg Frequently Asked Questions on Politically Exposed Persons," May 2008.

Table A1.2 (continued)

	UNCAC	FATF	Third EU Directive
Senior management approval	Not specified	Obtain senior management approval for establishing business relationships with such customers	Have senior management approval for establishing business relationships with such customers[e]
Source of wealth, source of funds	Not specified	Take reasonable measures to establish the source of wealth and source of funds	Take adequate measures to establish the source of wealth and source of funds that are involved in the business relationship or transaction[f]
Ongoing monitoring	Not specified	Conduct enhanced ongoing monitoring of the business relationship	Conduct enhanced ongoing monitoring of the business relationship[g]
General EDD	[...] conduct enhanced scrutiny of accounts sought or maintained by or on behalf of individuals... Such enhanced scrutiny shall be reasonably designed to detect suspicious transactions for the purpose of reporting to competent authorities....[h]	As above	As above

Source: Authors' compliation.
Note:
a. See FATF glossary.
b. Directive 2005/60/EC, Article 13(4).
c. Directive 2006/70/EC, Article 2(4).
d. Directive 2005/60/EC, Article 13(4)(a).
e. Directive 2005/60/EC, Article 13(4)(b).
f. Directive 2005/60/EC, Article 13(4)(c).
g. Directive 2005/60/EC, Article 13(4)(d).
h. UNCAC, Article 52(1).

Appendix D: United Nations Convention against Corruption (UNCAC) and Interpretative Notes

United Nations Convention against Corruption

Article 52
Prevention and detection of transfers of proceeds of crime

1. Without prejudice to article 14 of this Convention, each State Party shall take such measures as may be necessary, in accordance with its domestic law, to require financial institutions within its jurisdiction to verify the identity of customers, to take reasonable steps to determine the identity of beneficial owners of funds deposited into high-value accounts and to conduct enhanced scrutiny of accounts sought or maintained by or on behalf of individuals who are, or have been, entrusted with prominent public functions and their family members and close associates. Such enhanced scrutiny shall be reasonably designed to detect suspicious transactions for the purpose of reporting to competent authorities and should not be so construed as to discourage or prohibit financial institutions from doing business with any legitimate customer.

2. In order to facilitate implementation of the measures provided for in paragraph 1 of this article, each State Party, in accordance with its domestic law and inspired by relevant initiatives of regional, interregional and multilateral organizations against money-laundering, shall:

   (a) Issue advisories regarding the types of natural or legal person to whose accounts financial institutions within its jurisdiction will be expected to apply enhanced scrutiny, the types of accounts and transactions to which to pay particular attention and appropriate account-opening, maintenance and record-keeping measures to take concerning such accounts; and

   (b) Where appropriate, notify financial institutions within its jurisdiction, at the request of another State Party or on its own initiative, of the identity of particular natural or legal persons to whose accounts such institutions will be expected to apply enhanced scrutiny, in addition to those whom the financial institutions may otherwise identify.

3. In the context of paragraph 2 (a) of this article, each State Party shall implement measures to ensure that its financial institutions maintain adequate records, over an appropriate period of time, of accounts and transactions involving the persons mentioned in paragraph 1 of this article, which should, as a minimum, contain information relating to the identity of the customer as well as, as far as possible, of the beneficial owner.

Interpretative notes for the official records (travaux préparatoires) of the negotiation of the United Nations Convention against Corruption[74]

Article 52
Paragraph 1

49. The travaux préparatoires will indicate that paragraphs 1 and 2 should be read together and that the obligations imposed on financial institutions may be applied and implemented with due regard to particular risks of money-laundering. In that regard, States Parties may guide financial institutions on appropriate procedures to apply and whether relevant risks require application and implementation of these provisions to accounts of a particular value or nature, to its own citizens as well as to citizens of other States and to officials with a particular function or seniority. The relevant initiatives of regional, interregional and multilateral organizations against money-laundering shall be those referred to in the note to article 14 in the travaux préparatoires.

50. The travaux préparatoires will indicate that the term "close associates" is deemed to encompass persons or companies clearly related to individuals entrusted with prominent public functions.

51. The travaux préparatoires will indicate that the words "discourage or prohibit financial institutions from doing business with any legitimate customer" are understood to include the notion of not endangering the ability of financial institutions to do business with legitimate customers.

Paragraph 2
Subparagraph (a)

52. The travaux préparatoires will indicate that the obligation to issue advisories may be fulfilled by the State Party or by its financial oversight bodies.

Paragraph 3

53. The travaux préparatoires will indicate that this paragraph is not intended to expand the scope of paragraphs 1 and 2 of this article.

---

74. United Nations General Assembly, "Interpretative notes for the official records (travaux préparatoires) of the negotiation of the United Nations Convention against Corruption," (A/58/422/Add.1), paras. 49-53.

Appendix E: Financial Action Task Force on Money Laundering (FATF)— Recommendations, Interpretative Notes, and Methodology

Recommendation 6
Politically Exposed Persons

Financial institutions should, in relation to politically exposed persons, in addition to performing normal due diligence measures:

a. Have appropriate risk management systems to determine whether the customer is a politically exposed person.
b. Obtain senior management approval for establishing business relationships with such customers.
c. Take reasonable measures to establish the source of wealth and source of funds.
d. Conduct enhanced ongoing monitoring of the business relationship.

FATF "Glossary of Definitions Used in the Methodology"

"Politically Exposed Persons" (PEPs) are individuals who are or have been entrusted with prominent public functions in a foreign country, for example Heads of State or of government, senior politicians, senior government, judicial or military officials, senior executives of state owned corporations, important political party officials. Business relationships with family members or close associates of PEPs involve reputational risks similar to those with PEPs themselves. The definition is not intended to cover middle ranking or more junior individuals in the foregoing categories.

Interpretative Note to FATF Recommendation 6

Countries are encouraged to extend the requirements of Recommendation 6 to individuals who hold prominent public functions in their own country.

Methodology for FATF Recommendation 6[75]

The essential criteria and additional elements listed below should be read in conjunction with the text of Recommendation 6 and its Interpretative Note.

Essential criteria

6.1 Financial institutions should be required, in addition to performing the CDD measures required under R.5, to put in place appropriate risk management systems to determine whether a potential customer, a customer or the beneficial owner is a politically exposed person.

> Examples of measures that could form part of such a risk management system include seeking relevant information from the customer, referring to publicly available information, or having access to commercial electronic databases of PEPs.

6.2 Financial institutions should be required to obtain senior management approval for establishing business relationships with a PEP.

6.2.1 Where a customer has been accepted and the customer or beneficial owner is subsequently found to be, or subsequently becomes a PEP, financial institutions should be required to obtain senior management approval to continue the business relationship.

6.3 Financial institutions should be required to take reasonable measures to establish the source of wealth and the source of funds of customers and beneficial owners identified as PEPs.

6.4 Where financial institutions are in a business relationship with a PEP, they should be required to conduct enhanced ongoing monitoring of that relationship.

Additional elements

6.5 Are the requirements of R.6 extended to PEPs who hold prominent public functions domestically?

6.6 Has the 2003 United Nations Convention against Corruption been signed, ratified, and fully implemented?

---

75. FATF Anti-Money Laundering and Combating Terrorist Financing Methodology 2004 (updated June 2009).

Appendix F: Directives of the European Parliament and of the Council

Directive 2005/60/EC of the European Parliament and of the Council of October 26, 2005, on the prevention of the use of the financial system for the purpose of money laundering and terrorist financing[76]

Article 3

For the purposes of this Directive the following definitions shall apply:

(8) "politically exposed persons" means natural persons who are or have been entrusted with prominent public functions and immediate family members, or persons known to be close associates, of such persons;

SECTION 3

Enhanced customer due diligence

Article 13

1. Member States shall require the institutions and persons covered by this Directive to apply, on a risk-sensitive basis, enhanced customer due diligence measures, in addition to the measures referred to in Articles 7, 8 and 9(6), in situations which by their nature can present a higher risk of money laundering or terrorist financing, and at least in the situations set out in paragraphs 2, 3, 4 and in other situations representing a high risk of money laundering or terrorist financing which meet the technical criteria established in accordance with Article 40(1)(c).

4. In respect of transactions or business relationships with politically exposed persons residing in another Member State or in a third country, Member States shall require those institutions and persons covered by this Directive to:
   (a) have appropriate risk-based procedures to determine whether the customer is a politically exposed person;

---

76. Official Journal L 309, 25/11/2005, pp. 0015 – 0036.

    (b) have senior management approval for establishing business relationships with such customers;

    (c) take adequate measures to establish the source of wealth and source of funds that are involved in the business relationship or transaction;

    (d) conduct enhanced ongoing monitoring of the business relationship.

Commission Directive 2006/70/EC of August 1, 2006, laying down implementing measures for Directive 2005/60/EC with regard to the definition of "politically exposed person" and the technical criteria for simplified customer due diligence procedures and for exemption on grounds of a financial activity conducted on an occasional or very limited basis[77]

Whereas:

(5) Persons falling under the concept of politically exposed persons should not be considered as such after they have ceased to exercise prominent public functions, subject to a minimum period.

Article 2

Politically exposed persons

1. For the purposes of Article 3(8) of Directive 2005/60/EC, 'natural persons who are or have been entrusted with prominent public functions' shall include the following:

    (a) heads of State, heads of government, ministers and deputy or assistant ministers;

    (b) members of parliaments;

    (c) members of supreme courts, of constitutional courts or of other high-level judicial bodies whose decisions are not subject to further appeal, except in exceptional circumstances;

    (d) members of courts of auditors or of the boards of central banks;

    (e) ambassadors, chargés d'affaires and high-ranking officers in the armed forces;

    (f) members of the administrative, management or supervisory bodies of State-owned enterprises.

None of the categories set out in points (a) to (f) of the first subparagraph shall be understood as covering middle ranking or more junior officials.

The categories set out in points (a) to (e) of the first subparagraph shall, where applicable, include positions at Community and international level.

---

77. Official Journal L 214, 4/8/2006, pp. 0029 – 0034.

2. For the purposes of Article 3(8) of Directive 2005/60/EC, 'immediate family members' shall include the following:
   (a) the spouse;
   (b) any partner considered by national law as equivalent to the spouse;
   (c) the children and their spouses or partners;
   (d) the parents.

3. For the purposes of Article 3(8) of Directive 2005/60/EC, 'persons known to be close associates' shall include the following:
   (a) any natural person who is known to have joint beneficial ownership of legal entities or legal arrangements, or any other close business relations, with a person referred to in paragraph 1;
   (b) any natural person who has sole beneficial ownership of a legal entity or legal arrangement which is known to have been set up for the benefit de facto of the person referred to in paragraph 1.

4. Without prejudice to the application, on a risk-sensitive basis, of enhanced customer due diligence measures, where a person has ceased to be entrusted with a prominent public function within the meaning of paragraph 1 of this Article for a period of at least one year, institutions and persons referred to in Article 2(1) of Directive 2005/60/EC shall not be obliged to consider such a person as politically exposed.

Appendix G: Field Mission Survey— Questions for Banks, Regulators, and Financial Intelligence Units

Legislative/Regulatory Framework

Questions for Banks and Regulators

1. Please describe the legal and regulatory framework with regards to PEPs. Who is responsible for what?
2. How are PEPs defined in the regulations/legislation? (obtain copies of legislation/regulation)
3. What are the legal and/or regulatory obligations on financial institutions with regard to PEPs? Who else is covered? Who is exempt?
4. Do firms have access to further guidance on how to interpret the PEP obligations? If so, who issues this guidance and what is its status? How is it enforced?

Implementation of PEP Standards by Banks

Questions for Banks Only

Organizational Considerations

5. What are bank policies on PEPs? If applicable, do you have different policies for different geographic or business parts of your group?
6. How does your institution define a PEP? If your definition differs from the legislator's/regulator's, when and why did you decide to amend it? Did you consult with the regulator and what were the results?
7. How do you organize your PEP work (compliance, policy, etc.)? Is there a specific person or unit in charge of PEP issues?
8. What training and education is provided on CDD, EDD for PEPs, reporting? Who implements it? Who receives it? When is it delivered (frequency)? What does it cover? Are these functions audited by inside/outside auditors?

Procedures at Account Opening

CDD

9. Please describe your standard CDD policies and procedures with regard to the identification and verification of the customer and the beneficial owner. (If a form is used, we kindly request a copy of this form.) Will you adapt these policies and procedures to take account of different risk levels?
10. If you cannot verify the customer or the beneficial owner of a new customer, legal entity/account, what procedures are followed?
11. What activities can be carried out on behalf of the customer prior to completion of the verification process?

PEPs

12. Do you screen all customers for PEP purposes? Do you apply PEP checks to beneficial owners as well?

13. What steps are taken to determine if a customer is a PEP? When are these steps taken? What sources are used?

14. Do you maintain a list of your PEP customers? Who maintains this list and how often is it updated?

15. What procedures are followed once a PEP is identified (for example, risk assessment, source of wealth, source of funds, senior management approval)? How and when do these take place?

16. How do you determine the money laundering risk posed by a PEP customer or applicant for business?

17. Do you evaluate the reputation risk to your institution of corruption? How do you assess this risk? What steps are involved?

18. For those PEPs from countries where they must file a mandatory financial and business interest disclosure, do you request those disclosures before opening an account? If so, do you check whether the origin of the intended deposit can be identified in light of the disclosures? Do you ask for updated information on the same basis the government requires or on a different basis? How is the information provided on the form used?

19. Do you have or recall recent examples where a PEP was identified by the bank and the process/steps that were executed?

Existing Customers and Beneficial Owners

20. Do you run PEP checks on existing customers and beneficial owners?

21. What triggers such checks?

22. What procedures are followed once an existing customer or, if applicable, beneficial owner, is identified as a PEP?

Source of Wealth and Source of Funds

23. What steps are taken to establish the source of a client's wealth and the source of a client's funds?

24. In the event of doubts about the source of funds, what happens? Investigation? PEP contacted? Onsite visits?

Ongoing Monitoring

25. How are PEP transactions monitored?
    1. How do you determine the frequency of the monitoring?
    2. Manual or electronic monitoring used?

Unusual Transactions and Reporting of Suspicious Transactions/Activity

26. What are the policies and procedures for identifying and analyzing unusual transactions? Are there special procedures if a PEP is involved?

27. How do you decide whether a transaction involving a PEP account is suspicious?

28. When do you report?

29. What are the liability issues for reporting and failure to report? Tipping off?

Auditing

30. Do you regularly review CDD policies, systems and controls, and transaction monitoring systems in relation to PEPs? What does this process involve? If a profile/risk database is relied upon, how is this tested?

31. Have you come across any difficulties or issues? What recommendations do you have to improve how regulators and financial institutions address PEP issues?

Correspondent Banking and Financial Intermediaries

32. Do you check whether correspondent banks and financial intermediaries are adequately and effectively complying with CDD and EDD for PEPs?
33. Do you look at PEPs in the context of FATF designated nonfinancial businesses and professions?

General/Effectiveness

34. Where do you think the risks of PEP money laundering are the highest?
35. How effective do you think PEP controls are in preventing the laundering of proceeds of corruption?
36. What do you think are the main barriers to the effective implementation of PEP systems and controls? (for example, problems with the identification of PEPs (definition), lack of guidance, insufficient buy-in from staff)
37. What do you think could improve banks' compliance with PEP requirements?
38. What motivates banks to comply with PEP requirements? (for example, fear of sanctions, reputational risk, ethical considerations)
39. Is there coordination with other stakeholders in the private and/or public sector on the PEP issue?

Enforcement by Supervisory Authorities of PEP Standards

Questions for Regulators

Organizational

40. Please describe your approach to supervision (risk-based, compliance based, etc.). How do you allocate resources, and how do you determine the frequency of visits?
41. What is your role in relation to anti-money laundering and PEPs?
42. How is your work (on AML/PEP) organized?
43. Has the supervisor issued specific guidelines/manual that set out the regulatory expectations on PEPs? What happens if a firm does not respect these?
44. Did the supervisor draw up internal guidelines or instruction manuals to assist his/her personnel on how to assess PEP compliance?
45. Are all supervisors trained to assess a firm's PEP controls?

Supervision (On/Off-Site)

46. How do you organize AML/PEP assessments?
47. Do you systematically supervise compliance with PEP provisions in each inspection program and/or onsite visit?
48. Do you do targeted AML inspections? If so do you focus on PEPs? Have you ever considered doing a targeted PEP inspection?
49. Does the supervisor routinely collect information with regard to PEP identification, monitoring, and reporting (qualitative and quantitative) from banks? For example, are banks required to transmit to the supervisor copies of their PEP-related internal procedures? Who is responsible for analyzing these, and related, documents?
50. Does the FIU inform the supervisor about banks that are not submitting STRs and/or STRs on PEPs? If so, what steps are taken?
51. Does law enforcement inform the supervisor of cases involving PEPs? If so, what steps are taken?
52. How is the effectiveness of a firm's PEP systems and controls assessed? If a profile/risk database is relied upon, how is this assessed?
53. Who is responsible for preparing the onsite visit and selecting team members? How many people on average and what are their professional backgrounds? Do they take any PEP related training?

54. Is there any coordination between the off-site department and the onsite team prior to the onsite visit?
55. What kind of information/data is collected about the target bank prior to the visit, specifically in relation to PEP risks (for example, number of PEPs, number of PEP STRs?)
56. Which methodology do the onsite examiners rely on (get a copy)?
57. How do they assess CDD and KYC; PEP identification, risk assessment, and monitoring; and STR compliance? What is the depth of their examination?
58. What is the exact scope of the PEP onsite inspection? Do examiners examine (i) compliance with national regulations? (ii) adequacy of internal organization, IT equipment, and internal monitoring tools? (iii) quality or effectiveness of PEP identification (effectiveness of databases, sources relied upon)?
59. How do examiners select the files or areas of activities to be assessed? (Please explain scoping and sampling process.)
60. Beyond the examination of files, is there anything else that is routinely done to assess compliance?
61. Do examiners obtain a copy of STRs filed and sent to the FIU? If so, do they examine the quality of the report?

Reporting

62. Does the supervisor maintain statistics on findings? For example, on the quality of PEP controls? If so, how are these statistics being used?
63. What are the common PEP compliance failures?
64. When PEPs or PEP STRs have been identified by examiners, what steps are taken?
65. Does the FIU receive a copy of the inspection reports or at least some excerpt?

Follow-Up

66. Where you have identified problems with a firm's PEP controls, do you follow up? What are your options?
67. Are serious failures in PEP compliance communicated to the FIU?

Regulatory Actions

68. Do you consider breaches of PEP obligations to be serious?
69. What kind of regulatory actions can the supervisor apply to a financial institution that failed to comply with PEP requirements (scope)?
70. Are sanctions adequate and deterrent?
71. Are all rulings given by the competent authorities routinely published, and if so, in which document (annual report, official government gazette)?
72. Which authority is responsible for sanctioning (the supervisor, a court, the FIU)?

Effectiveness

73. Where do you think the risk of PEP money-laundering is highest?
74. How effective do you think PEP provisions are in deterring or detecting the laundering of proceeds from corruption?
75. What do you think are the main obstacles to the effective implementation of the PEP provisions?
76. Based on your supervisory work, how would you assess overall levels of compliance with the legal/regulatory PEP requirements?
77. What could be done better/what is missing?
78. Is there coordination among stakeholders in the private and/or public sector?

Role of FIU in Supporting Implementation of PEP Standards

Questions for FIUs

79. What is your role in relation to AML/PEPs (if applicable, beyond that of a FIU)?
80. Have directives been issued to financial institutions to explain how to report PEP STRs?
81. Can you identify PEP-related STRs? If so, how? Do you recommend the use of a check-box on the STR form?
82. How are PEP STRs processed and analyzed?
83. How are PEP-specific reports produced? How are they shared with investigation or prosecution agencies?
84. Do you maintain statistics on PEP STRs?
85. Do you produce PEP typologies, PEP threat assessments, or other information to support firms in their compliance with legal and regulatory obligations?
86. Does the FIU inform the supervisor about banks that are not submitting STRs and/or STRs on PEPs?
87. Is there coordination among stakeholders in the private and/or public sector?

National and International Cooperation

Questions for Banks, Regulators, and FIUs

National Cooperation

88. What kind of cooperation has been established so far on PEPs and PEPs STRs with national authorities (for example, the FIU, the police, customs, and other financial institutions/supervisors)?
89. How is the cooperation facilitated? (Memorandum of Understanding/multidisciplinary teams)? What is the process?
90. Are there any restrictions on the ability to exchange information between national agencies?
91. What is the relationship between the supervisor and the FIU?
92. What is the relationship between the supervisor and the law enforcement agencies, including prosecutorial authority?

International Cooperation

93. What kind of information sharing and cooperation is there with foreign affiliate financial institutions and correspondent banks?
94. What kind of cooperation has been established so far on PEPs with foreign supervisory authorities or FIUs and law enforcement agencies?
95. How is the cooperation facilitated? (Memorandum of Understanding?)
96. Are there any limitations on the type of information that can be exchanged with foreign authorities? (Please provide examples.)

Index

Boxes, figures, and notes are indicated by *b*, *f*, and *n* following the page numbers.

Eco-Audit

Environmental Benefits Statement

The World Bank is committed to preserving endangered forests and natural resources. The Office of the Publisher has chosen to print *Politically Exposed Persons* on recycled paper with 30 percent post-consumer waste, in accordance with the recommended standards for paper usage set by the Green Press Initiative, a nonprofit program supporting publishers in using fiber that is not sourced from endangered forests. For more information, visit www.greenpressinitiative.org.

Saved:
- 8 trees
- 3 million BTU's of total energy
- 804 lbs. CO_2 equiv. of greenhouse gases
- 3,876 gallons of wastewater
- 235 lbs. of solid waste

green press INITIATIVE